T0309802

The Efficient Practice

The Efficient Practice

Transform and Optimize
Your Financial Advisory Practice
for Greater Profits

DAVID L. LAWRENCE

WILEY

Published by John Wiley & Sons, Inc., Hoboken, New Jersey.
Published simultaneously in Canada.

For general information on our other products and services or for technical support, please contact our Customer Care Department within the United States at (800) 762-2974, outside the United States at (317) 572-3993 or fax (317) 572-4002.

Wiley publishes in a variety of print and electronic formats and by print-on-demand. Some material included with standard print versions of this book may not be included in e-books or in print-on-demand. If this book refers to media such as a CD or DVD that is not included in the version you purchased, you may download this material at http://booksupport.wiley.com. For more information about Wiley products, visit www.wiley.com.

Library of Congress Cataloging-in-Publication Data:

ISBN 9781118735039 (Hardcover)
ISBN 9781118735145 (ePDF)
ISBN 9781118735152 (ePub)

Printed in the United States of America
10 9 8 7 6 5 4 3 2 1

I would like to dedicate this book to the most inspiring person in my life, my mother, Helen Mattson Lawrence. Helen was an amazing educator for over 60 years, founding her own private school in Florida and pioneering groundbreaking visual teaching techniques for what was referred to then as minimal brain dysfunction children (later called dyslexia). She lived a full life, passing at age 90. But she never lost her love or her enthusiasm for teaching children.

—David L. Lawrence

Contents

PART TWO

Technology Efficiency

PART THREE

Process Efficiency

PART FOUR

Design Efficiency

Introduction

As professionals, financial advisors have been very well educated on how to be a financial advisor, but the profession has done a poor job of preparing financial advisors to be great business owners. This is due in part to the industry's focus on licensing and certification, not to mention compliance-related issues.

Financial practices often grow from a single-person firm to a larger firm with challenges in several key areas of operations. Some firms reach a point that might be termed a *revenue ceiling*. This is a level of net profit above which the firm cannot seem to grow. Adding more employees, purchasing additional equipment, or even increasing marketing to new prospective clients does not solve the problem as the firm is constrained by its operational construct and management. Firm owners frequently do not recognize the issue because most often they are the problem themselves.

The solution is to take a holistic approach to all areas of financial practice operations and use efficient management techniques to create systems that can greatly extend net profitability, productivity, and efficiency.

I developed a concept many years ago that I call Profit-Driven Architecture, which is a visual way of viewing the operational structure of a financial practice. Regardless of whether it is a small or large firm, the structure provides a concrete way of understanding and improving the interrelationship of different parts of the operations of a financial practice firm. (See Figure I.1.)

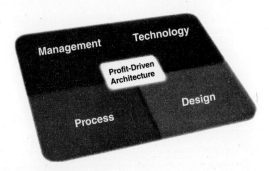

FIGURE I.1   Profit-Driven Architecture

Each of the four areas of firm operations should be studied to find ways to increase the efficiency, productivity, and profitability of the firm. However, these areas of operations do not function independently. The greatest impact in efficiency is achieved when these are studied holistically, recognizing the interrelationships with each other. As an example, management efficiency must be studied in the context of how well technology and process relate to the management of the firm, and so on.

The Efficient Practice explores the tools and techniques to bring a firm above the revenue ceiling and achieve the highest possible levels of efficiency, productivity, and profitability. Other impacts to the firm can be increased capacity and a significant rise in practice value. Given an aging population of financial advisors and increased focus on succession planning, increasing the value of a financial practice is a key deliverable of efficiency.

David L. Lawrence

The Efficient Practice

PART One

Management Efficiency

CHAPTER 1

The Efficient
Management Philosophy

One of the great challenges of management is adjusting to the growth of a firm. The adjustment is not confined to the owner/manager. Adjustments must be made by all members of the firm. Clearly, though, the first and most fundamental step is for the owner/manager of the firm to recognize that as the firm grows, he or she must change the way in which management of the firm is handled.

For most practitioners who began as a one-person shop, this is a difficult task. When operating a one-person shop, the owner does it all, from clerical to analytical. When the first employee is added, there is still little need for formal management techniques, as there may be time to discuss most everything. But, as more and more employees are added, there is an inefficiency of scale that sets in, interfering with work productivity, increasing time demands on the owner/manager, and potentially limiting profitability. Often referred to as a revenue ceiling, this is the point in growth where the limitations of management so hinder the efficient operations of the practice that continued revenue growth becomes virtually impossible without major changes.

Similar in scope to the law of diminishing returns or the law of increasing opportunity costs (originating with eighteenth- and early-nineteenth-century economists such as Thomas Malthus and David Ricardo), increases in gross revenue could be outpaced by exponential increases in the cost of doing business. One firm recently reported that they were adding new employees at the rate of two a year to keep pace with increased workload, yet their net revenue number continued to remain the same as before (or to slightly decline). Bringing on more clients, increasing asset management (AUM) fees, and creating new recurring revenue sources also did not seem to help the bottom line. The discouraged partners were seriously considering breaking the firm apart and downsizing.

When a practice efficiency analysis was accomplished, several things came to light (four of which are mentioned here). First, the company was operating as a *modified silo* firm. This is where each of the five partners essentially ran their own operation. But, an attempt had been made to integrate staff to some degree. This created a boondoggle for employees, who were asked to adapt on a daily basis to five different styles of doing business.

Second, most reports (quarterly investment reports, for instance) were taking each of four staff assistants around eight hours (per report per staff member) to prepare. This is because the source data was coming from multiple locations (different software, websites, etc.) and had to be manually integrated into a single document. Often the resulting document had mismatched fonts, pagination, formatting, and styles.

Third, management style was somewhat myopic in structure. There was an office manager charged with running the office, but with little authority to actually manage the employees. If he was given the task of assigning work, many times, one or another partner would go around the manager to assign additional unrelated work to the same employee, requesting priority.

Fourth, there was no formal workflow process and follow-up procedure in place. With a lack of workflow and/or task completion standards (time and quality), there was no structural methodology for evaluating employee and/or manager performance. With close to 30 employees, this firm was attempting to run itself using the same techniques as a much smaller firm, and it simply was not working.

In short, this firm was badly in need of a management philosophy that would permeate each and every area of practice operations. It is not enough to state the philosophy or even print it in a manual; it must be a philosophy that lives and breathes with every activity within the firm.

COMMUNICATION IS KEY

One of the key skills that should be incorporated into a management philosophy is communication; communication with clients is important, but communication with employees is critical. Where communication fails, so does the practice, operationally speaking. Micromanagement creeps in and things grind to a halt.

Much has been written about leadership and efficiency. Some have suggested that leadership should be *systematic and disengaged* from process (*Financial Advisor*, March 2007, Editor's Note, ". . . worked on his practice, never in it"). Yet, day-to-day activities form the lifeblood of a financial practice. Therefore, the challenge for leaders (managers) of a practice is to determine to what extent they should play a role in those activities without crossing the line to micromanagement. At the opposite end of the spectrum is the strategic leader, who eschews daily responsibility in favor of a visionary role.

Typically, the financial advisor who runs his or her own practice wears a number of hats: manager, analyst, salesperson, marketer, public speaker, and family person, to name a few. Depending on the size of the financial practice, staff may assist with some of these roles. This places emphasis on the role of manager. Yet, the same financial advisor may also be active in technical roles within the firm. Possessing both technical and managerial skills is daunting, to say the least. Add to that the skills of a public speaker, and you have a nearly impossible combination of skill sets.

Given that challenge, it might be prudent to consider more efficient ways of carrying out the various roles demanded of the financial advisor. First, the role of leader/manager should be considered. Albert Einstein once said that "creativity is 10 percent inspiration and 90 percent perspiration." (The same or similar quotes have been attributed to Thomas Alva Edison and others.) The same can be said of leadership. It can also be said that 90 percent of a leader's activities are in the realm of communication and 10 percent comprises everything else. If we accept this notion, then it suggests that a small improvement in communication skills could lead to a more efficient advisory firm.

Consider the four communication styles of leadership shown in Figure 1.1.

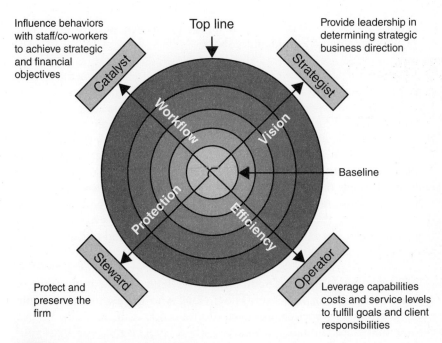

FIGURE 1.1   Four Faces of Leadership
Source: Adapted from Breathing Lessons #7, © 2007, Deloitte Development, LLC.

The reality is that leaders must possess the chameleon-like ability to assume all four of these communication styles when appropriate. No one style may be perfectly appropriate, though. The fact that this chart appears like a target is not by accident. Where a leader may find her point on this target may be due to a blending of two or more of these styles and in consideration of the task at hand. Workflow should be handled within the larger context of the vision of the firm. In addition, protecting the firm must be balanced against the needs (and risks) associated with achieving firm-wide goals. Ultimately, this chart illustrates the delicate balancing act a leader must follow to be successful. Efficiency is driven by how well the leader can function within this environment without being bogged down by the details.

To be most efficient in your role as a leader, leadership must be shared with those who are led. Delegating tasks is one thing; delegating responsibility is quite another. In order to be most efficient in accomplishing the goals of your financial practice, eventually you will need to embrace the concept of delegating responsibility. To be consistently successful in this, three steps must be accomplished:

1. Matching responsibility to the appropriate person and assessing readiness levels
2. Holding that person accountable for the expected results
3. Following up and providing feedback

Assessing readiness levels is a skill unto itself. Often, staff members may feign proficiency to prop up their value to the firm. Do not assume that just because someone says he knows how to do something that he actually does. A manager must be capable of cutting through the hyperbole and ascertain the specific readiness level of a staff member prior to assigning tasks and/or responsibilities. This might be accomplished by simply asking questions like, "When you say that you know how to do this, perhaps you could briefly take me through the steps involved…" or words to that effect. Assigning responsibility also involves motivating that person to do a good job. Placing the importance of the task or set of tasks in the larger framework of importance to the firm or clients can accelerate completion and efficiency more than top-down commands such as "because I said so."

Accountability is another key step in delegating responsibility. Holding people accountable for their actions speaks volumes on the importance of setting high standards in a firm. Those of us who are parents understand that the first time we let children get around a rule is the last time we can enforce that rule. Though it would be folly to suggest that you treat your staff like children, there are those inevitable comparisons. While we are on the subject, what is accountability? *Accountability* should mean that there are consequences to one's actions. This can mean good or bad consequences (reward vs. punishment). Rewards can come in many forms, such as additional privileges, bonuses, and so on. Punishment can be as subtle as the removal of authority (responsibility) or as overt as withholding bonuses or reduction of pay or worse. The degree would be determined by the egregious nature of the situation. To work, the criteria must be objective, fair, and consistently applied. They must also be discussed well in advance.

Follow-up is the third step in delegating responsibility and is perhaps the most important. Yet, it is often the most neglected step. Ironically, it could be the easiest to accomplish using technology. Most client (customer) relationship management (CRM) software packages, scheduling software, and calendars offer the ability to track tasks in one way or another. Scheduling a follow-up with a staff member should be a habit that is done at the same time a task or responsibility is assigned. Some advisors have developed the additional habit of having the affected staff-person place the follow-up on their calendar as well. In this way, that person recognizes the importance the advisor (manager) places on follow-up and feedback.

Following up on task and/or responsibility delegation is as important as what is being followed up on. Do not overly complicate the follow-up communication. Keep focused on the issue and simplify the communication as much as possible. Even though it may be dated material, consider using the *One-Minute Manager* (© HarperCollins, 2000) style of feedback by pointing out the strengths of the individual in the task and the areas for improvement going forward.

Consider the value of introspection. Hold yourself accountable for your tasks and responsibilities. Ask what consequences you will suffer for not accomplishing those tasks or fulfilling those responsibilities. In addition, determine what rewards you are due for meeting or exceeding your own expectations. Recognize that you are being judged not only on how efficiently you manage others, but also on how well you manage yourself.

THE IRONY OF MICROMANAGING

Given that there are financial advisory firms that struggle with the growth of their practices, a simple phrase comes to mind: *You cannot grow until you let go.* Many firms began as one-person shops and grew from there. However, in many cases, the firm continues to be managed as though it was still a one-person company, with one person involved in all aspects of firm operations. As a firm experiences growth, this becomes an unworkable management model and actually can limit or prevent growth from occurring.

Typical characteristics of micromanagers include:[1]

- They believe that being a manager means that they have more knowledge and/or skill than their employees.
- They believe they can perform most of the tasks of their staff, probably better.
- They believe that they care about things (quality, deadlines, etc.) more than their staff.
- They feel it is more efficient to do the job themselves than give the job to a staff member.
- They are overly critical of their staff. When they review the work of staff members, they tend to find at least one thing wrong each time. (They often suffer from "red pen" syndrome.)
- They don't allow their staff to learn from their mistakes.
- They get irritated if staff makes decisions without consulting them.
- They spend an inordinate amount of time overseeing single projects.
- They pride themselves on being on top of their staff's projects.
- They are overworked, and their staff is not.
- They come into the office earlier than any staff member and leave later. If they are away from the office, they call in at least twice a day, including when they are sick or on vacation.
- They seldom praise staff members.
- Their staff appears frustrated, depressed, and/or unmotivated.
- Their staff does not take initiative—they have to check with the manager before doing anything.
- They have been referred to as controlling, dictatorial, judgmental, critical, bureaucratic, suspicious, or snooping by staff, managers, or family members.

The following story illustrates at least some of these points.

Some years ago, on a visit to a financial advisor's office, I noticed a 10-minute egg timer sitting on the advisor's desk. It was a sand-filled hourglass-type of timer. I asked the advisor what that was for. He said with a smile, "Oh, that. That is my workflow management system." I asked how it worked. He explained, "I turn this thing over and when the ten minutes are up, no matter what I am doing, even if I am sitting with a client, I get up from my desk and go around to each one of my employees to see what they are doing and what I can do to help. And, I do this because I am a river to my people."

---

[1] Global Knowledge Whitepaper, 2011.

Needless to say, his employees did not feel the same way about this workflow system as he did. Upon examining the employee records, it was found that the firm "enjoyed" a 50 percent annual employee turnover rate. With only seven employees, this was quite significant and inherently inefficient. However, there was one employee who had been there for over seven years. A part-time employee who did accounting work, she was clearly the most vocal against the boss. Calling him an insufferable micromanager and several other names that cannot be repeated here, I asked why, if she felt so strongly, she was still there. She looked me straight in the eye and said, "It makes you wonder why I married the man."

This same firm was experiencing what is commonly called a revenue ceiling. This is a level of net profitability above which the firm cannot seem to attain, despite significant efforts to do so. The firm owner was either unwilling or unable to see the detrimental effects his management technique was having on the firm, much less the limiting factor on firm growth and profitability. And, as surprising as this scenario might seem, it is far from unique. Many firms are experiencing similar restrictions on profitability and growth owing at least in part to their style of management.

Two possible root causes of micromanaging could be attributed to either poor management skills or poor leadership skills. In the management area, it could be that:

- The manager still views himself or herself as a *doer* versus an *overseer.*
- The manager may be an expert in a certain field, or have a personal passion for a particular specialization, which makes it difficult for him to step back from the details.
- The manager will not, or does not know how, to delegate. He seems to struggle to get the work done that his staff "couldn't or wouldn't finish."
- The manager will not, or doesn't know how to, coach. She doesn't take the time to help her staff learn.
- The manager cannot manage projects effectively. He requires frequent communication with his employees, including detailed status reports and updates.
- The manager has difficulty managing her time. She spends her time immersed in the staff's projects instead of performing her management functions.
- The manager has difficulty managing pressure from above or from outside the organization.
- The manager can get lost in the details and not take the time to see the forest through the trees. This could include spending too much time on mundane tasks such as reading e-mails, Internet surfing, and so on.

In the leadership area, it could be that:

- If a manager has been held accountable for the failings of his staff in the past, he may find it difficult to trust the skills/knowledge of current staff.
- If a manager has been let down by staff in the past, he may be cautious about trusting the word and/or motivation of current staff.
- If a manager has developed personal control issues to satisfy internal needs, this may be expressed by the need to appear the most knowledgeable; by difficulty in sharing information or credit; or by the need to gain a sense of power from feeling "needed" by others.

Here are five steps to overcome being a micromanager:

1. **Admit it:** The first step to losing the label is admitting you may have micromanagement tendencies. This means that you admit it not only to others but, most important, to yourself.
2. **Solicit feedback from your managers and staff:** Once you recognize that you may be a micromanager, you will want to figure out if your actions are harmful to you and your staff or merely necessary for greater good of the organization.
3. **Identify the root cause of your micromanagement tendencies:** If you find that you display tendencies that are causing harm in your relationships with your staff and potentially making you an inefficient member of the organization, you may want to explore the causes of your micromanagement.
4. **Seek advice, guidance, and training:** Once you are more aware of the root cause of your micromanagement style, you will be able to seek the advice, guidance, and training necessary to change.
5. **Develop an automated workflow system:** With automated task assignments, easily tracked completion status, and reporting tools, the manager can step back from the micromanagement role. (See Part Three for more details.)

DELEGATE, DON'T DOMINATE

A true workflow management system can and should contain three elements of control: *assignment*, *accountability*, and *documentation*. If employed within a software-type environment, these three can be highly developed and observed by management without constant oversight or micromanagement. Studies have shown that when workflow management systems are properly applied, consistency, firm growth, and firm capacity can be significantly increased. Time management can also be improved and, perhaps most important, tasks are far less likely to fall through the cracks.

It is curious that, although perhaps hundreds of books, articles, and websites are devoted to time management, most of us still struggle with this critical skill for financial advisors and business owners. A recent Google search using the term *time management* produced 228 million listings. Certainly there is an abundance of information on this subject, perhaps even too much. Yet, poor time management represents the single most expensive aspect of running a financial advisory practice.

One reason might be that many solutions to time management involve linear approaches to solve the problem. As an example, if it is discovered that an advisor is spending an inordinately large amount of time answering and writing e-mails throughout the day, suggestions to solve this might include setting aside a specific time (or times) during the day in which e-mails might be handled. Yet, is this always going to be the perfect solution? Not if the advisor should *not* be handling the e-mail in the first place or if certain e-mails should be filtered out or redirected to another staff-person.

Linear thinking involves cause-and-effect types of activities. If you do *this*, then *that* happens, and so on. And, while this may be an effective approach in some areas, it may not be the most efficient way of dealing with time management issues. The problem stems from trying to standardize a process with an issue that often cannot be standardized. Each situation, when encountered, could call for different approaches. And this strikes at the heart of the problem. Most advisors who began as one-person shops and were required to do it all for themselves may find that once the practice grows and employees enter the picture, it becomes difficult to relinquish control or to effectively delegate (knowing when and how to delegate). When a firm owner tends to try to handle it all, things frequently degrade into crisis mode: handling the problems as they arise, especially when they present themselves as overwhelming in importance (at least insofar as the financial advisor may perceive it). *Reactive* time management versus *proactive* produces time management nightmares. It effectively means loss of control of the advisor's schedule. And, it is often so debilitating that the advisor could be paralyzed by it.

Not surprisingly, those advisory firms that struggle with time management also struggle with clutter. Clutter is a key symptom of poor time management. In those practices where clutter is prevalent, poor time management is very likely to exist as well. This is because those who tend to clutter do not have the methods in place to deal with paperwork efficiently, and thus the piles grow until the situation reaches the crisis stage. At this point, the advisory practice may find it necessary to literally shut down the office for a day or two to clear out the piles and restore order.

Procrastination, especially with respect to running a financial advisory practice, can only lead to disorganization, stress, and even chaos. Therefore, it is extremely important to overcome procrastination, particularly with respect to time management. But, ultimately, how can a firm gain control of time and still operate at a high level of efficiency, productivity, and profitability? One way is to move beyond linear approaches to solving such problems and embrace *adaptive strategic thinking* as a logical alternative.

Adaptive strategic thinking (AST) involves a different decision dynamic with respect to issues such as time management. In AST, decisions might be made based on situational criteria, with multiple channels of support, avenues of solutions, or choices to make. Any one of the choices made could potentially solve the problem at hand; the challenge is finding the optimal approach or combination of approaches. Cause and effect still applies, but in a multidimensional decision hierarchy, the optimal approach may involve situation-specific decision parameters that utilize multiple resources and/or techniques.

An example of the difference between linear thinking and adaptive strategic thinking can be found in the military. In Vietnam, soldiers were asked to fight an enemy they could not identify (because they often wore the same clothing as civilians) with weapons and techniques that were developed during World War II, when military campaigns were carried out on a traditional battlefield, versus jungle warfare and/or kids carrying bombs in flower baskets on the streets of Saigon. There were no lines of soldiers facing down each other (except in rare cases). Most fighting was with sniper fire, hidden bomb devices, and an elusive enemy that traveled in tunnels. To properly confront such an enemy, the U.S. military had to adapt to a totally different style of fighting. This meant more than just training and uniforms. It meant employing different weapons, using technology, and gaining the trust of locals. Much of this is still true with what the military has had to deal with in Iraq and Afghanistan. It short, it means addressing challenges with a willingness to change multiple variables to achieve optimal results. And, it also means being willing to adjust those variables as situations present themselves.

Taking the concept into the financial advisor's office, one relevant example of how this might work is in our earlier example in this chapter regarding e-mails. The linear approach might be to set apart a specific time out of each day to read and answer e-mails. The adaptive strategic approach might be to look at the preponderance of e-mails over a given length of time, and determine the statistics on how many of those might have been filtered out altogether, how many could have been handled by a staff-person, and how many had to be dealt with by the advisor. Then, technology might be employed to sort the incoming e-mails according to their priority and handling. When using most CRM programs with e-mail capabilities or Outlook, there are Rules Wizards that can catch an e-mail upon receipt and move it into a specific folder. In an enterprise server environment, this could mean parsing out e-mails in the order of importance, who handles it, subject or category, priority, or any number of those variables applied simultaneously. You may also be able to automate the copying of e-mails into special folders for compliance and/or archival purposes. The result could be a much simpler, easier-to-navigate inbox for the advisor with only those e-mails he or she really needs to see.

What is important to recognize is that no technology can ever take the place of critical reasoning. Therefore, other staff must be trained to review their folders and react to those one-off situations in which an e-mail was redirected into a folder but really did need the attention of the financial advisor. The adaptive thinking aspect of this is to account for and recognize the value of staff training to uncover and respond appropriately to those types of situations.

While the handling of e-mails is only one aspect of time management (phone calls, file handling, paperwork disposition, compliance reporting, and client appointment scheduling being just a few of the others), using adaptive strategic thinking in all areas of time management offers the best chance to gain control of the financial advisor's time and optimize the efficiency of the financial practice.

As an example, on a recent visit to a financial advisor's office, observation was made of this firm owner typing initial entry data into financial planning software. In calculating the income of this advisor, expressed as an hourly amount, the equivalent hourly wage worked out to $450. So, this begged the question of this advisor, "Would you pay an employee $450 per hour to enter names, addresses, phone numbers, and the like?" When the answer was an emphatic *no*, the observation was that this is exactly what he was doing. So the question for the rest of us is: "What are you doing?"

There are three key questions that should be asked:

1. What are you doing that you should be doing?
2. What are you *not* doing that you should be doing?
3. What are you doing that you should *not* be doing?

Finding the answers to these questions goes way beyond simple time management and task delegation, and addresses the issues of collaborative endeavor and appropriateness of responsibilities.

One way to diagnose this is to keep a log of all of your activities during the course of the typical workday. While at first this might seem to be an annoying exercise, it may force you to realize what it is you really do with

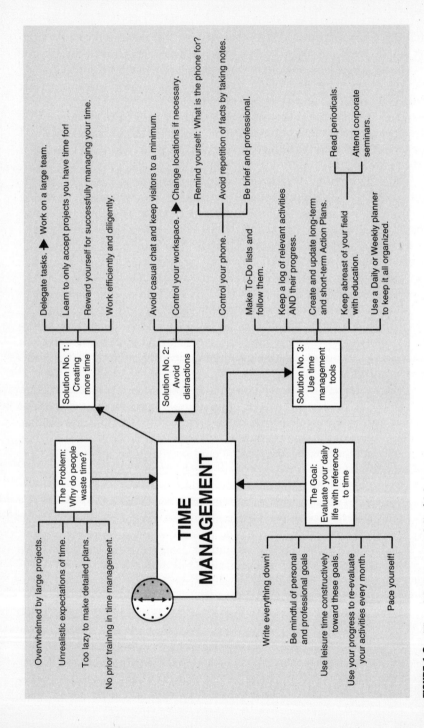

FIGURE 1.2 Time Management Mind Map

your time during the course of a day. And you may only need to do it for a week or so to truly reveal what you are doing with your time.

Another approach is to use mind mapping software to think through the time management issues that you might have in your work. A typical example of such a mind map is shown in Figure 1.2.

Many financial advisors use mind mapping with their clients to help think through the issues confronting their financial future. However, mind mapping can be a useful tool to help think through the issues associated with a financial advisor's daily activities.

Once the activities have been identified, you may wish to apply some financials to drill down to the appropriateness of the person doing the activity, whatever it may be. This can lead to the process of collaborative endeavor.

Collaborative endeavor is, or should be, a process of questioning to be successful. With having more than one person sharing responsibility, there is first the question of feasibility. Is it feasible to have multiple hands on a project, task, or workflow? And how do the assignments of work get done?

Next, there is the question of strategy. How does the endeavor compare to other collaborations? What intrinsic value does this endeavor offer as distinct from others? What differences will it make to participate in this endeavor that give it advantages over others or leverage to motivate essential participants?

Finally, there is the question of efficiency. How much will get done through the endeavor? How quickly will it get done? How much involvement by how many people will it take to meet those targets? How vulnerable are the collaborative processes to breakdowns, rework, and schedule slippage? How many resources need to be tied up, and for how long, by the work getting done?

Once you have figured out the strategic goals of a collaborative endeavor, the next logical step is to develop workflow task sets. A *workflow* consists of a sequence of connected steps. It is a depiction of a sequence of operations, declared as work of a person, a group of persons, an organization or staff, of one or more simple or complex mechanisms. Therefore, having established workflows that consist of a series of established steps (or tasks) that lead to a completion and can be tracked in some way by management is a key way to increase efficiency through a delegated process without loss of control by the financial advisor or manager.

The value of established workflows is the ease with which they can be overseen and managed. If you go to the effort of establishing workflows with task sets, staff assignments, and managerial reporting and then micromanage the process, you will have accomplished nothing. Worse, you may do more harm than good. The purpose of a properly designed workflow management system is to relieve the firm owner or manager of overt management, permitting that person to focus on what he does best and/or what he needs to be doing.

Appropriateness of responsibilities is a difficult concept for financial advisors to grasp as many started their careers by doing everything. Delegation of tasks thus becomes difficult even with the growth of a financial practice.

There is a concept called the *revenue ceiling*, which is the net-profit point that a financial advisor's practice cannot seem to break above, despite bringing on new employees, buying the latest technology, and so forth. It is generally because the financial advisor cannot seem to break the habits he or she developed as a single practitioner. In many cases, it boils down to the appropriateness of responsibilities and, to some extent, placing trust in your staff to do the tasks assigned to them accurately, efficiently, and without constant monitoring.

The revenue ceiling effect can be overcome, but usually not by yourself. It requires a third-party perspective—someone from the outside offering objective solutions to break the bad management habits of the advisor relative to the management of his or her practice.

Passive management is a difficult concept for a hands-on type of person used to overseeing everything. However, passive management techniques must be mastered to optimize a financial practice's operational efficiency.

With respect to workflow task sets, utilizing CRM software that has workflow capabilities is a big help. With the typical CRM optimized for financial practices, there may be reporting capabilities that permit the firm owner or manager to surreptitiously view all the tasks and workflow progress throughout the firm, pinpointing overdue tasks as well as spotting tasks done ahead of schedule. And the beauty of these programs is the ease of obtaining the information without constantly questioning employees on what they may or may not be doing.

Delegation of important tasks to staff is empowering to them. It demonstrates your confidence in their abilities and your trust that the job will get done and done right. Micromanagement has the opposite effect. It tells your staff that you do not trust them to get it done right. And, it can lead to higher levels of employee dissatisfaction and staff turnover (which can be expensive to the firm).

To ensure that task delegation is done right, communicating effectively on what is entailed in the task (or set of tasks) is critical. Following-up after the fact, pointing out areas of proficiency and improvement needs, is also critical. Most important is to delegate those tasks that you should not be doing. Financially, it is the right thing to do, and it will ultimately lead to higher levels of efficiency in a financial advisor's practice.

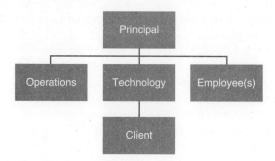

FIGURE 1.3   Standard Organization Chart

Creating an efficient client relationship model should also be part of your overall management philosophy.

Management structure is also a key issue in communicating who does what and why. Violating management structure can lead to chaos, lack of respect (on the part of your employees), and more. The organization chart in Figure 1.3 suggests a common organizational model.

The client-centric model might look more like the one in Figure 1.4.

FIGURE 1.4   Client-Centric Model

The concept is that every decision, every part of your firm is filtered through the question, How does this benefit my client? Applying this model to a concierge-style of practice, the firm would feature:

- Casual open environment
- Client-centered (client-centric)
- Provider of services (in-house or outsourced)
- Positioned to be first call for client needs

The advantage of such a style of doing business is in your clients' perception of what you can do for them. Here are some typical added services:

- Mortgages
- Tax preparation
- Auto lease-versus-buy options
- Travel planning
- Business planning

Most of such services would be *outsourced*, with your affiliation partners meeting with your clients in your office. Retaining control of your clients' financial decisions and representing the first point of contact with your clients for *any* financial issue is the goal of adding this laundry list of concierge-style services.

Creating a management philosophy is more than just a statement in a book or strategic plan. It should be the basis for a structural concept that permeates every aspect of business operations and is easily understood and followed by everyone in the firm. Communicating this philosophy to your clients can be a relationship-strengthening aspect of your client engagements and can lead to higher levels of referrals. It can also result in greater operational efficiency, productivity, and profitability.

SUMMARY

In Michael Gerber's books that explore the *e-Myth*, he talks about the business owner being either a technician or an entrepreneur. Many firms begin as a one-person shop, with that one person being the technician who does it all. With firm growth, inevitably things have to change. The technician owner needs to morph into an entrepreneur and work on the business, not necessarily in the business. This transition has proven to be difficult, if not impossible, for some firm owners, as they do not have the skills or experience in the new role of entrepreneurship to turn to when needed. For this reason, considerable thought and planning need to be undertaken as the firm grows to make this transition work well.

Adopting an efficient management philosophy should be the first step. And, in making this step, the firm owner needs to recognize some of the key skills that need to be mastered in order to apply this philosophy to his or her financial practice. Two of those skills are critical to success: communication and delegation.

Communication can best be summed up as two-way understanding. The communicator is assured that whatever is said is understood by those receiving the communication. In the financial services profession, this is absolutely a must if the firm is to do its work, transact business, process paperwork, effect trades, and manage money with a minimum of errors and/or misunderstandings. The simple fact is that errors can cost money—a *lot* of money.

In Stephen R. Covey's book, *The 7 Habits of Highly Effective People* (Free Press, 1989), the fifth habit is "First seek to understand and then be understood." This is a critical aspect of managing people as some firm owners assume they are being understood, without taking the time to ensure that is true. And, while employees may possess high skill levels at certain tasks, it should never be assumed that they have equal skill levels for all tasks that they may be asked to perform. For this reason, it is incumbent upon the firm owner to ascertain the level of understanding and the skill level of the person they are communicating with in order to assure that whatever the task at hand is, it will be completed successfully and with a minimum of errors or delays.

The second skill is delegation, often a stumbling block for those firm owners who have trouble letting go (micromanagers). This chapter discusses techniques to delegate efficiently and effectively. A true workflow management system can and should contain three elements of control: assignment, accountability, and documentation. If employed within a software-type environment, these three can be highly developed and observed by management without constant oversight or micromanagement. And using technology tools to observe workflow activity can actually strengthen relationships with employees by giving a heightened appearance of autonomy in fulfilling their duties within the limits of responsibility.

Finally, the chapter discusses the differences between *linear* and *adaptive strategic thinking* (AST). The skills employed in using AST can create higher levels of productivity in an environment that fosters flexibility to changing conditions.

Managing Resources

For the record, an *efficient practice* is often defined as one that maximizes profit for the given resources at its disposal. *Efficacy* is defined as the power or capacity to produce a desired result (i.e. effectiveness). Efficacy is neutral on efficiency. That is, it is possible to be effective, while being inefficient. As an example, suppose you provide an outstanding financial plan to your client. The client derives great benefit from the plan, but it took you (and/or your staff) an inordinately large amount of time to complete it. You might consider the delivery of the plan and client's need as more important than the efficiency of delivering the product to the client.

EFFICIENCY VERSUS EFFICACY

It is also possible to be efficient while also being largely ineffective. Simply pumping out products or work without considering the value to one's clients could create such a situation.

Herein lies the paradox of financial advisory practices. Are those practices in place to provide outstanding services at any cost, or are those practices in business to make money? The irony of this paradox is that, though seemingly opposing concepts, *efficiency* and *efficacy* can work hand in hand. In other words, you *can* have your cake and eat it, too. To accomplish this, a financial advisory practice would first need to assess the efficiency level of the office and staff to determine to what extent improvements need to be made. A few questions that a practice might consider exploring are as follows (the point of the questions is to evaluate to what extent the statements are true):

1. I/we have technological systems that share data seamlessly and provide benefits of efficiency in entering information only once.
2. I/we use software systems and other means of automating compliance responsibilities, including but not limited to electronic file storage and retrieval, letter templates, and other advertising venues.

3. I/we prepare an annual business plan and check it frequently through-out the year to ensure I/we are on track for our goals.
4. I/we use a time schedule template to ensure that sufficient time is set aside to accomplish all tasks and appointments from week to week (and I/we follow it religiously).
5. I/we have prepared up-to-date procedures manuals for each and every task-oriented position in the firm.
6. I/we use our office space to its maximum efficiency given our space limi-tations.
7. The employees of my/our firm are the best people for the jobs they per-form (all of them).
8. I/we have a company website that is truly interactive with constantly updated content and client usability features.

Though the above list of eight statements is far from all the issues associated with efficiency, it should suffice to begin the process of evaluating how you do business.

One of the key statements on our list is #3, the one that deals with a business plan. Many firms create business plans, but often fail to use them as an efficient yardstick on their progress. As an example, suppose a restaurant has a really great turnout of diners for a holiday such as Valentine's Day one year, but fails to use that information to adequately prepare for next year. This could leave the restaurant short of needed staff, supplies, or even sufficient food to serve. Restaurants frequently use projections in their business planning to assure that sufficient resources are in place to meet needed demand for services. Financial advisory prac-tices could borrow a chapter from the restaurant business plan process by considering the value of the ongoing use of a properly prepared busi-ness plan.

Financial advisors need to not only prepare business plans, but also compare business results with those plans as an ongoing planning process to ensure that expected growth projections meet with results. Often, in this planning approach, the financial advisor should consider starting with the end in mind. Determine a realistic *net profit* number for a given year ahead. Emphasis is given to net profit, as gross numbers tend to skew thinking on how the firm is really doing. Net profit reveals the efficiency of business planning. Yes, it is a harder target to reach, but a more satisfying one when it is reached.

The process might be compared to a *reverse P&L statement*. This is where the bottom line becomes the top line and all the details fall below. If you work through a broker/dealer and have B/D concessions, fees, and other expenses to consider, the example shown in Table 2.1 might apply.

TABLE 2.1   Reverse P&L Statement

	2011	2012	2013	2014
Net Profit	$ 27,900	32,085	36,898	42,432
Expenses	$ 52,300	60,145	69,167	79,542
Rent	$ 14,000	16,100	18,515	21,292
Wages	$ 20,000	23,000	26,450	30,418
Computer related	$ 3,000	3,450	3,968	4,563
Software license fees	$ 2,500	2,875	3,306	3,802
Office supplies	$ 750	863	992	1,141
Membership in assoc.	$ 350	403	463	532
Technology access	$ 1,200	1,380	1,587	1,825
Advertising/marketing	$ 3,000	3,450	3,968	4,563
Postage/mail/shipping	$ 500	575	661	760
Legal fees	$ 300	345	397	456
E&O insurance	$ 4,000	4,600	5,290	6,084
Other insurance	$ 500	575	661	760
Equipment leases	$ 1,200	1,380	1,587	1,825
Misc. other	$ 1,000	1,150	1,323	1,521
Adjusted Gross Profit	$ 80,200	92,230	106,065	121,974
B/D concession	$ 15,000	17,250	19,838	22,813
B/D association fee	$ 4,800	5,520	6,348	7,300
Gross Revenue (GDC)	$ 100,000	115,000	132,250	152,088

Source: Copyright ©2014 David Lawrence and Associates.

The net profit number for 2011 in Table 2.1, though somewhat appallingly low in this example, illustrates the purpose of designing a reverse P&L statement. It shows the importance of net profitability. We can sometimes fool ourselves into thinking we are doing well when all we look at is gross revenue. But, the reality is found in the net profit number. In this example, it is hard to imagine how the practitioner could financially survive. Yet many advisors have spreadsheets that look similar to this.

By taking the 2011 numbers and applying a 15 percent increase in successive years, we can use this spreadsheet to show the effect on net profit should the practice experience a 15 percent increase in business. Over the three-year period shown, for instance, net profitability rose by 66 percent.

The spreadsheet shown in Table 2.1 could also be used, where multiple-year data is available, to better understand some of the expense numbers, such as advertising and marketing expense. In years where higher levels of advertising/marketing were done, what impact did that have on the net change in net profit? It might provide an objective basis for determining marketing spending levels (or even the type of marketing) in future years.

Using the same line of reasoning, it might be inferred that a similar conclusion could be reached with wages. Often practices respond to increasing workloads by adding additional staff. This decision may be made without consideration to overall profitability. We might justify the decision based on workloads and providing timely services to clients. However, did the same decision result in lower overall profits, and is that a decision we would have made had we known the outcome in advance?

Another point to be made regarding this concept of a reverse P&L statement is reflected in the expenses number. Often, financial advisors believe that the only way to increase profitability is through either increasing business (bringing on additional clients) or cutting expenses. But this ignores the possibility that profitability could be increased by simply doing more with the expenses you already have. By developing systems and using firm resources more effectively, you and/or your staff can increase capacity. That is, your practice can handle more business with the same staff and equipment levels. With no additional costs, any new clients and/or assets added to the practice will translate into higher net profit.

But a reverse P&L statement is only the beginning. Just looking at numbers does not address the specifics of cost controls that ultimately could improve those numbers. Cost controls applied to a financial advisor's practice can embrace a number of different disciplines, from quality control studies to Six Sigma practices. With respect to the latter, *Six Sigma* is a set of practices designed to systematically improve processes by eliminating (or at least minimizing the negative impact of) nonconforming product or service offerings. Applied to financial services firms, this might utilize a set of five basic methodology steps identified as *DMAIC*:

1. *De*fine the process improvement goals that are consistent with client needs and firm strategy.
2. *M*easure the current process and collect relevant data for future comparison.
3. *A*nalyze to verify the relationship or causality of factors. Determine what the relationship is and attempt to ensure that all factors have been considered.
4. *I*mprove or optimize the process based upon the analysis using techniques such as workflow study comparisons (comparing the same process performed by different people in your firm).

5. Control to ensure that any variances are corrected before they result in profit dampening. Set up and run oversight procedures and measure control mechanisms to ensure consistency.

Though the specific techniques of Six Sigma go way beyond this simple acronym, it serves to illustrate the systematic approach to address process management and improvement in your firm. The term *sigma* is derived from the statistical function of standard deviation. In a cost control study, sigma typically refers to the number of standard deviations between the average time (for example) to complete a particular process and the nearest process specification limit.

To illustrate, let us say that in the inputting of a financial plan (FP) by an employee of a firm, management assumed that it would take, on average, about three hours to complete the data inputs. But in studying a firm with several employees who are responsible for such a task, it became apparent that most of the plans were taking about four hours to input. In a statistical bell curve, the study of this might look like the chart in Figure 2.1.

This chart reveals that most of the time the data inputs seem to be accomplished in or around four hours. However, there is one employee who managed to get the job done in less than two hours and another who took nearly seven hours to complete. Certainly, this would be valuable information to the owner of the firm as it could uncover a highly efficient employee (or one who is cutting too many corners), and it could also uncover a training

FIGURE 2.1   FP Input Hours by Employee

opportunity for the employee who is identified as taking too long to get the job done.

Another application of this chart is in identifying the norm or average time to complete a task. If a task takes on average four hours to complete, then the firm has a basis upon which to objectively determine the productivity of a particular employee as it relates to a specific workflow task. It also permits the firm to set limits on what is deemed acceptable performance (perhaps, in this illustration, a range of three to five hours). Anything outside that range might be cause for management concern.

The overwhelming reason to embark on such studies is to determine if the firm is getting the biggest bang for the buck. Does it make sense to pay two employees the same where one takes twice as long to complete the same set of tasks? Does it matter to the firm if the employee who takes half as long to complete a task is making so many mistakes that, ultimately, it takes longer to finish due to corrections, costs the firm money due to mistakes, and/or forces management intervention, wasting even more time? These are the sorts of questions that cost-control studies can answer. And by applying such a technique to the management of a financial advisor's practice, the impact is likely to be higher levels of net profitability, efficiency, and success.

OUTSOURCING

Most financial advisors reach a point in their practice where they realize that they cannot do it all, much less manage it all. Specializing in different aspects of the profession becomes more reasonable and cost effective when outsource solutions to fill the gaps can be located and employed. If there is one profession that has responded to this need, certainly it is the financial advisory profession. There are tons of outsource solutions and resources for advisors to consider—so much so, that discerning which ones fit the needs of a particular practice can be difficult, if not confusing.

For the sake of reducing the confusion, providers of outsource services could be divided into two categories. The first might be called *niche providers*. These would be providers of specific types of services, such as outsourced receptionist duties, financial plan preparation, or portfolio management services. The second category might be *comprehensive* or *all-in-one* providers.

Niche providers have gained in popularity in recent years. While there are too many to list here, a couple of worthy providers to note might be in the area of portfolio management. Back Office Support Service, better known as BOSS (www.thebackoffice.biz), is a full-service outsourcing firm providing web-based portfolio management systems, fee billing and client reporting services, daily reconciliation, and a host of related services. In an interview with President and CEO Mike Kelly, he described it this way:

> *BOSS takes care of the daily data management, report generation, and fee billing, so financial advisors can focus on what they do best—servicing their clients! Our outsourcing model provides an alternative for advisors who want cost-effective expertise for their reconciliation, performance calculations, and other portfolio management service (PMS) related tasks. We work in partnership with the advisors to ensure the PMS software enhances their business operations, adds efficiency, and provides sound information for their decision making and communication to clients.*

BlueLeaf (www.blueleaf.com/advisor) provides simplified client reporting and portfolio management services and provides a web-based client portal for clients to review their investments, performance, and details on their holdings, and offers a collaboration technology for advisors to use with their clients and other professionals.

In yet another area for niche providers, unrelated to portfolio management, virtual receptionist services can potentially save a smaller firm hundreds every month while providing a high-quality service. One particular company in this category to note is Ruby (www.callruby.com). Ruby is comprised of a smart and cheerful team of virtual, live receptionists trained to make a difference in your office's operations. From their studio in Portland, Oregon, they handle your calls with friendliness, charm, can-do attitude, and professionalism. Best of all, your callers will think they work in your office. Ruby answers the calls and then transfers those calls, as applicable, to wherever you may be. With pricing plans ranging from $229/month to $769/month, those costs will be far below what you might have to pay for an onsite person.

Another firm worth checking out in this same category is Onebox (www.onebox.com). Onebox is an all-in-one virtual phone solution featuring an auto-attendant, professional greetings, voicemail, online faxing, and conference calling, allowing you to easily manage all business communications. While not as personable as a live attendant, such as with Ruby, Onebox provides a low-cost virtual solution with prices starting around $50/month.

In the area of comprehensive, holistic outsourcing solutions, two (among many) firms might be worth checking out. The first is Focus Point Solutions (www.focuspointsolutions.com). Focus Point allows advisors to outsource all of the following: reporting, trading, billing, and even your investment process and research. Additionally, they offer a technology platform, compliance solutions (including Registered Investment Advisory [RIA] services formation), and strategic guidance and transition support. In an interview with Chris Hicks, president of Focus Point, the question was asked, "What is the new focus of Focus Point Solutions?" Chris replied that in recent years they have focused on rebuilding their infrastructure. In doing so, they took a step back to look at the client relationship management (CRM) software that might be supported. They decided, two years ago, to go with a customized version of Microsoft Dynamics CRM and have worked hard to develop this customized version for their advisors. In fact, rather than attempt a one-size-fits-all approach, Focus Point has committed to customizing each advisor's version of Dynamics to fit the needs of that particular firm.

In adopting the Microsoft platform, they chose to use SharePoint for document sharing and collaboration. And, they integrated the use of other providers such as LaserApp and MoneyGuidePro and portfolio management systems such as Advent. Chris mentioned that the 400+ advisory firms they support are mainly fee-based businesses, and Focus Point has positioned itself as a broker/dealer alternative. The reason, he pointed out, is because broker/dealers have been forced to raise fees and other costs due to the rising compliance requirements, and, with potential fines going up, smaller firms are finding it tougher to align with the broker/dealers. Thus, the search for less expensive alternatives might lead them to Focus Point.

A second comprehensive solution worth a look is BAM Advisor Services, LLC (BAM) (www.bamadvisorservices.com). BAM cut its teeth on the CPA markets, working with accountants who were interested in expanding into the investment arena. However, BAM's focus has shifted (or perhaps expanded) to now include RIA-type firms. Consequently, their services have also expanded to include firm development and growth services such as practice development, client recruitment programs, and advisor coaching. Their technology platform continues to evolve. BAM has recognized that the one-size-fits-all approach is untenable in the financial services profession, and has embraced a number of supported systems and technologies as a result. BAM also offers a large laundry list of client services, including portfolio management, risk management, retirement plan services, analysis support services, and communication resources such as educational materials, quarterly newsletters, whitepapers, and PowerPoint presentations. They partner with such firms as DFA Funds, Schwab, and Fidelity to offer choices for advisors.

In trying to determine if one or more outsource solutions are right for your firm, it is wise to do your homework. Doing a cost-benefit study, with comparisons to the costs incurred by providing those same services in-house, could be revealing. However, it is also important to fairly weigh differences in the client service experience and what impact that might have on your practice. Ultimately, the goal may not be simply to save money, but a combination of providing a higher level of service with lower costs and outsourcing certain aspects of your financial practice that you either do not do well or would rather not do, freeing you to focus on those things that you do well. For some advisors, this translates into more face time with the client. For others, it may mean freeing up existing staff from mundane tasks to concentrate on higher-level (analytical) work without constant interruptions. In either case, if chosen wisely, outsourcing should result in a more efficient and productive financial practice.

DOWNSIZING

Given that the past few years or more have been financially challenging for most financial advisors, some have chosen to downsize in an effort to regain profitability. Yet, without a clear plan to downsize, you could be doing more harm than good in the long run.

In a recent conversation with a financial practice in New York State, the decision had been reached to move into a smaller office space, downsizing the office from 1,500 square feet (SF) to 1,200. And, while the rental area was less (300 square feet less to be precise), the costs may not have been. In the larger space, the office was rented for $12/SF/year. This amounts to $18,000/year of office rental cost (not including extras, taxes, etc.). The new space cost $13.50/SF/year. While not that much more per SF, the apparent cost savings with the smaller space per year is $1,800 (again, not including extras). Over a four-year span, the cost savings would amount to $7,200.

On the surface, it looks like a good deal. However, if we take into account the cost of the move, roughly $5,750 in this example, along with the cost associated with a change of address (letterhead, envelopes, business cards, Yellow Pages listings, advertising, and more), then the cost savings quickly evaporates. And, if we factor in the time cost associated with packing, moving, and setting up the new office, and multiply that times however many employees are involved, instead of being a cost savings the move actually cost more than if the firm had stayed where it was.

In the end, the firm in this example is faced with additional expenses and no cost savings for having made the move, and it now must function with significantly smaller office space. Plus, the aggravation, confusion, and frustration associated with making a move leads to employee discontent and client dissatisfaction. Ultimately, what does it say to your clients when you move into a smaller, cramped space?

Having said all this, there are times when moving into another location does make sense. There have been financial advisory firms that were partnerships where the partners chose to break up. In this instance, making the move can be explained to clients in a logical way. And, with significantly less staff (for instance) continuing to operate in a much larger office that is only half-full can be unsettling to the clients of your firm. In other words, moving into a smaller office space is justified for more than just the cost factors.

Reducing the size of the office is just one of the many issues that can be addressed in downsizing. Some firms have chosen to downsize the number of employees. And while the cost associated with payroll is generally one of the highest in a firm, this is often mishandled, resulting in not only the loss of a valued employee, but the loss of trust of the remaining employees.

Yes, there are situations in which an underperforming employee can be identified and weeded out, as was the case recently with a firm in Tennessee where one of the highest paid employees was found to be perusing NASCAR websites on the company computer most of the day rather than contributing to the success of the firm. In another case in Texas, a new male employee was caught viewing porn on a company computer in full view of anyone (including clients) who might walk by his desk. These are obvious employee termination circumstances that would not necessarily be isolated to downsizing situations. The tougher calls are the ones where it is determined due to the firm's loss of revenue from percentage fees for assets under management (AUM; due to a down-market condition) that one employee must be let go, when all employees are hard-working, talented, and motivated contributors. It is a tough call because the reasons for firing the employee may be unrelated to her job performance, attitude, and/or motivation.

To combat this, some firms have looked at firm-wide salary rollbacks as an alternative to releasing a valued employee. As an example, a firm could introduce a 10 percent rollback on a firm with seven employees that have an average salary of $40,000 each. This would free up $28,000, plus FICA, Medicare, state and federal tax withholding, 401(k) contributions, and potentially other costs in the budget. Ultimately, such a rollback could save the employer close to the cost of a single employee while firing no one. To counter the possible negative reaction from the employees to a rollback, it could be presented as a temporary cost containment procedure that is preferable to letting someone go. It could also be paired with a year-end (or quarterly) bonus program that is directly tied to net-profit increases, giving the employees the incentive to assist in making the firm more profitable as it could recover their 10 percent or more in the long run.

Yet another target of downsizing is clients. Some firms actually decide to downsize their clients, especially those that are viewed as time and/or labor demanders while contributing little or no profit to the firm. Many firms have a list of clients that were perhaps carried over from earlier years in the business. They may be substantially below (in assets, products, or other aspects) the ideal client for the firm. In some cases, they remain clients in name only, due to the limited nature of the relationship. Yet, they may be receiving the same level of support, feedback, reporting, access to their advisor, and so on, that the wealthier (or more appropriate) client is receiving.

In most cases, performing a cost-benefit analysis of your client base is an excellent way of determining the characteristics of your clients that provide the firm with the most efficient net profitability. And, while there are always exceptions (for example, a relative of a client), focusing on those clients that match up best with what you do and how you do it can improve the overall profit picture. The question is, what do you do with the others? Do you simply fire the clients that don't fit the ideal? Do you charge them more or reduce services to them? Do you assign them to the new advisor in the office for practice? These are the questions that must be answered. Whatever you decide to do, it must be explained to those clients in a way that is both positive and affirming.

Finally, there is one other aspect of downsizing to be considered, deciding what to do or not do in your practice. Trying to be all things to all people rarely works well. The old phrase, *Jack of all trades, master of none*, applies here. Beyond being impractical to present yourself as an expert in all areas of financial services, it is hugely inefficient to attempt to be that expert. Therefore, many firms have studied what they do well and what they do not do as well. Choices in this area are to either eliminate certain services or outsource those services that the advisor does not like to do, want to do, or do well. Some of the outsource areas to consider are financial planning, investment management and reporting, tax preparation, marketing, and advertising.

If handled prudently, thoughtfully. and efficiently, downsizing can right-size your practice and your profits.

MANAGING CHANGE: A PROCESS OF INCLUSION

Consider this scenario: You walk into your office one day carrying a book and your employees groan, roll their eyes, and make snide remarks about change coming to the office. If this has happened to you, it is likely because change has been mishandled in the past. The analogy of a boss reading new books (or attending conferences) and then imposing frequent, office-altering changes is common in financial practices. The scenario should more aptly be described as *change mismanagement*. The negative effect on the firm could be devastating in the long run.

Most office employees resist change. It requires a new learning curve. It means a loss of productivity during the learning phase, and it means disruption of daily activities. Therefore, unless there is an overwhelming reason for change, most employees will be uncomfortable with it. Some employees not only resist change but actively fight it. In cases where change is imposed, employees may feel threatened by change. This may be a reaction to a loss of control or a perception that their job is going to go away once the change is put into place. For this reason and others, implementing change in an office environment requires careful preparation and sensitivity to the perception of those who will be affected by it.

You cannot sell change to your employees. Selling change to employees is not a sustainable strategy for success. When office workers listen to the boss selling them on some revolutionary new way of doing things, most will smile and appear to accept the news, but quietly to themselves are thinking, "No way is this going to work."

Change needs to be understood and managed in a cooperative environment. Instead of selling change, the owner or manager should be focused on being a settling influence as change is introduced. Firm owners and/or managers need to check that people affected by the change(s) agree with or at least understand the need for change, and have a chance to decide how the change will be managed and be involved (in one way or another) in the planning and implementation of the change.

What if change needs to be made quickly? If change is needed quickly, the first step is to probe the reasons why. Is the urgency real? Will the effects of agreeing to a more reasonable timeframe be more disastrous than trying to push through a quick (and potentially disastrous) change? Quick change often leads to problems later, including but not limited to employee acceptance and adherence. Change of any sort needs to be fully explained and justified in order to get buy-in.

For most change to be successful, creating a sense of ownership is necessary. The simple fact is that conventional organizational change, which typically involves training and development (and *motivation*), frequently fails. It fails because employees look at things differently from owners and managers. Some bosses actually believe that people who are paid to do a job should do what they are told to do. Imposing change on people doesn't work because:

- It assumes that the employees' personal aims and wishes are aligned with those of the organization or that there is no need for such alignment.
- It assumes that the employees want the type of change that the firm deems appropriate for them.

Instead of imposing change on your employees, you should consider exploring ways to align the aims of the business with the needs of your employees. This does not mean that because you consulted with your employees before and during change, you are handing over the firm to them. The reason to consult with your staff is that it saves you from yourself and your own wrong assumptions. Consulting with them gives you and them a chance to fully explore and understand the implications and feasibility of what you think needs to change. And it gives your employees the opportunity to see things from both sides and may just open the door to better ideas for doing things than you could have thought up all by yourself. In fact, it helps *you* to see from both sides, too.

Often, organizations have enacted change without fully engaging the employees in the process because they perceive that there is not enough time to reassess and realign aims and values or that change is a response to some crisis. Crisis, though, is no excuse for compromising integrity or short-circuiting respect for the views of your employees. Crisis should be a wakeup call to enact change carefully and is the best reason to realign your aims and consult with your staff on that change. When a firm is in crisis mode, the employees are almost always okay with doing what it takes to "right the ship."

How do you enact change? Change should be handled as a project and managed accordingly. This means developing the conditions, variables, and consequences of change. It also means enlisting your employees in the process of change through a thoughtful, considerate schedule that takes into account what needs to be done to successfully enact the change, given the limitations and schedule implications for those employees who will ultimately have to deal with a transition. Project management takes into account a series of activities that lead to a successful outcome or change in the firm.

Building a project requires some skill. Apart from using project management software, there are practical considerations to incorporate into the planning process. Four steps might be considered in the process.

1. *Setting goals* is usually the first, most logical step. What do you hope to accomplish with the change in your office? When do you hope to accomplish it? This might involve a strategic planning type of meeting with staff to develop ideas and share insights. Using a third-party consultant, for instance, to facilitate discussions with staff on change can further distance you from the negative role of persuader.
2. *Setting the roles and responsibilities* usually comes next. Who is responsible for what, and how do you set accountabilities?
3. *Setting a timeline* for successful completion of the project, for instance, could be the third step. Whether or not you develop advanced Gantt charts that illustrate the timeline, success does not depend on fancy graphics, but on simple, clear communication of the timeline.

4. The final step should be to *set up a measurement system* to determine how successful the firm is in making the change(s) and whether the result matched the expectations.

Involving your staff in every step of the process of change will greatly improve the chances of success. Try to remember before enacting change that *change for the sake of change alone is largely useless.* To be successful, a firm does not need to jump on every new trend or idea that comes around. Carefully evaluating those trends or ideas in light of a firm's vision, values, and the resulting benefit to the client goes a long way toward determining the validity of making a change.

SUMMARY

Managing resources for a financial advisory practice involves many aspects of that firm's operations. Yet often it is the least-worked-on area of the practice. This may be due in part to financial advisors' focus on the client. While this may seem like the proper approach, you cannot offer services to clients if you go broke trying to do so.

This chapter explores the value of doing cost studies to identify how resources are being used and to uncover areas of operations where resources, including human resources, are being misused. The concept of a reverse profit-and-loss statement (P&L), where the bottom-line net profit becomes the top line, is intended to focus attention on the net profitability and the cost of doing business.

For some firms, the cost of certain aspects of firm operations cannot be justified when solely performed in-house. For those firms, outsourcing is a viable alternative to consider. There are a host of different providers to choose from when considering outsourcing some aspects of a financial advisors business. Some advisors turn to outsource providers once they recognize that they cannot do it all themselves. Outsourcing is a viable way to reduce costs and potentially provide higher levels of service. Caution is urged in selecting an outsource provider, as some may not be a perfect fit for the way the advisor's practice works.

This chapter also explores the inherent difficulty of micromanagement and the inevitable higher costs and lower revenue results. The chapter reviews ways to identify if you are a micromanager (often micromanagers are unwilling to admit this even to themselves). It also outlines ways to overcome this tendency and be more of a delegator with the result being a more harmonious workplace, greater levels of efficiency, better employee relationships, higher levels of job satisfaction, and lower employee turnover rates.

Finally, the chapter reviews ways to effectively downsize a practice, when downsizing is called for. Downsizing may better be referred to as *rightsizing*. In some cases, downsizing can actually result in higher levels of net profit. By focusing the practice in a narrower area of client needs, for instance, it may result in marketing and onboarding clients who are better suited to the skills and services offered by a particular financial advisor. And, by trimming staff, you may find that the result is higher levels of productivity, especially when the staff reduction is tied to outsourcing or downsizing a part of the client base that can be identified as less profitable or more time and resource demanding.

Properly managing the resources of a firm, all of them, can and should result in higher levels of efficiency, productivity, and net profitability. Trying to be all things to all people can often result in a service structure that has gaping holes or is unable to sustain consistent financial results. And, with higher employee turnover rates, dissatisfied clients, and inefficient operations, the financial advisor's practice can turn into a financial quagmire. Therefore, efficient management of a firm's resources is a key aspect of improving firm operations and profitability.

CHAPTER 3

Managing People
and Communications

Certainly among the key resources in any firm are the people who work there. Understanding first how to hire the right people and then manage those same people goes a long way toward effective use of human resources.

There is nothing more inefficient or costly than selecting the wrong person to fill a particular position within a firm. There is the time lost in the process, not to mention the cost, of acquiring a new employee along with wages paid to someone who does not stay. And, even though much has been written on the subject of employee selection, there are still a large number of firms that struggle with this concept. Most often, it is due to a lack of research and preparation prior to the hiring process, but it could be due to a variety of factors such as ill-defined job responsibilities, lack of attention to the team dynamics, personality issues, and other factors. And some firms have hired *targets of opportunity*. These are people who came to the attention of the firm, who possess certain skills, but may or may not be a good fit for the firm. So, what are the proper steps to ensure that the person you hire turns out to be the right employee?

STEP ONE: PRE-HIRE PREPARATION

Clearly, you cannot hire the right employee if you do not know who or what you are looking for. Having a fairly well-defined idea of who it should be will go a long way to finding this person. One way to accomplish this is with detailed position descriptions. By this, we are not talking about a one- or two-paragraph description, but a detailed list of position responsibilities, firm accountabilities, and management expectations. These position descriptions can be used not only in the hiring process, but also in periodic objective job evaluations. By establishing objective criteria, and then observing performance and behavior, the evaluation process is an objective-driven process rather than a subjective one.

Another aspect of the pre-hire preparation is in identifying where your job candidate could come from. For this, it will be necessary to determine the position requirements (i.e., education level, years of experience, and experience with certain aspects of the job). This will help to narrow down the sources of candidates. There are a number of firms that specialize in recruiting candidates for positions. With apologies to the many firms who offer such services, here are three worth noting: Turning Point, Inc. (www .tpisearch.com) assists in identifying veteran advisors and executives for the financial services profession, and New Planner Recruiting (www .newplannerrecruiting.com) works with college and university programs to identify appropriate financial planning practitioners. Experienced Advisor Recruiting (www.experiencedadvisors.com/) offers advanced services for firms specifically looking for experienced (5+ years), credentialed (CFP, CFA, AIF, etc.) financial planning and investment advisory professionals where firms need the unique blend of technical expertise and relationship management skills these advisors possess.

Use of these firms often comes at a price, but it may be worth it, considering the time and effort it takes to identify candidates and narrow the field to your firm's specific needs. There are also college programs with online graduate resumes for review.

STEP TWO: BACKGROUND INFORMATION

There are three sources of background information that are critical to the hiring process. First, you should consider putting your top candidates through some sort of psychometric testing. But this alone is not enough. You should first familiarize yourself with the test results, and you should also consider performing psychometric tests on all of your existing employees to create a team profile. This can aid in identifying who would fit in with the rest of the team. Knowing what test results would identify the perfect candidate for your position will give you an edge when your candidates do the test. Two companies that produce reliable results are Kolbe (www.kolbe.com) and Caliper Corp. (www .calipercorp.com).

Additional pieces of background information that should be gathered are criminal background reports (all U.S. states, not just your state) and, if applicable, U-4 information (SEC broker check, etc.).These days, such reports are easy and relatively cheap to obtain online. In most cases, for criminal background checks, you will need the candidate's permission and his or her Social Security number along with possibly other identifying information.

The resume is yet another source of background information. Apart from calling former employers, look for gaps in the history of employment. This can raise questions to be covered in an interview. When calling former employers, it is often difficult to get much info, but verifying employment and employment dates is helpful.

STEP THREE: THE INTERVIEW

This is also a critical step and is often mishandled by employers. The interview should be an objective set of questions that relate to work in general and the position offered in specific. The questions should be the same for each candidate so that an objective comparison can be made. And consideration should be made of the psychology behind the answers. The interview is the candidates' opportunity to show their best side and not necessarily reveal their shortcomings. To that end, one of the first questions that might be asked is, "Did you have any trouble finding us today?" If they answer that they did, it may be an indication that they did not do their homework on where the firm is located. This leads to the second question, which should be, "Tell us what you know about our company." What you hope to hear is that they visited your website, looked at other sources, and have a reasonable first impression of the firm and what it does. If they indicate that they really do not know much about the company, this should raise a red flag.

Some of the questions should explore hypothetical situations. An example of such a question is, "If you know that your boss is 100 percent wrong about something, how would you handle the situation, and what would you say to the boss?" The answer to questions like this may offer insight to the candidate's communication skills.

In asking such questions, look for more than just the verbal answers. Look at the nonverbal cues. Look for such cues as eye movement, pauses, and even Adam's-apple movement prior to or during a candidate's answer. According to studies, the Adam's-apple-jump is an unconscious sign of emotional anxiety, embarrassment, or stress. During an interview, for instance, a listener's Adam's apple may inadvertently jump should he dislike or strongly disagree with a speaker's suggestion, perspective, or point of view. One interesting source of information on this is the Center for Nonverbal Studies (http://center-for-nonverbal-studies.org/).

A longstanding goal of nonverbal research has been to find reliable signs of deception. The quest is fueled by popular and scientific observations that deceit often is accompanied by unconscious signals revealing anxiety, stress, or shame while lying. Studies indicate that certain signs used when speaking (for instance, a glance downward and/or rate of head and hand movements) accompany lies. Care must be taken not to misread these signals, as an overly nervous candidate could produce similar symptoms.

It is important to recognize that no one method is going to give you the best profile of a candidate. All of the previously mentioned sources of information need to be considered to provide the best verification of a candidate's qualifications and fit for the firm. And, if done methodically and consistently, the firm stands the highest likelihood of finding and retaining the right employee.

Compensation can often prove to be a difficult aspect of hiring and managing employees. With firm consolidation, such as advisors creating team practices, or advisors moving to independence and/or creating Registered Investment Advisory (RIA) practices, designing a compensation plan for yourself and those who might be working with you is one of the most fundamental steps in the change management process.

There would seem to be unlimited ways in which to set up a compensation plan, so the question becomes how a firm should decide which one is right for it. The answer lies in a thorough understanding of what the firm's strategic goals are and what sort of compensation incentives are important given the specific talent, skill level, and motivation of the individuals involved in the plan.

DEVELOPING A COMPENSATION PLAN

There are six logical steps to follow in the development process. These steps should be followed in the order shown to gain the most benefit from the development process.

1. **Evaluation:** Conduct a comprehensive evaluation of existing compensation plans, practices, or company-generated ideas and develop a feedback report of the findings.
2. **Compensation philosophy:** Define the company's compensation philosophy, which defines how and with whom the company intends to compete for its human resources and how and under what terms its advisors and/or employees will be rewarded. Typical choices might include fixed compensation (salary-based) versus variable compensation models (percent of AUM fees, percent of gross dealer compensation, percent of commissions, trails, recurring fees, etc.). In most cases, it will be a unique blend of some or all of these elements that will best match the firm's philosophy.
3. **Position analysis:** Conduct a comprehensive position analysis to determine the primary functions, duties, and responsibilities of all affected

positions. This analysis serves as the framework for developing market pricing. A comparison should be done with industry standards. A thorough understanding of each affected firm member's unique contribution to the success of the firm should be accomplished in this analysis.

4. **Administration guidelines:** Develop a market-based salary/bonus/incentive structure and compensation administration guidelines for setting pay and for adjusting compensation based upon performance, promotions, changes in job content, specializations, and changes in market rates of pay.

5. **Incentive and bonus plan(s):** When appropriate, develop an incentive and/or bonus plan (or plans), based upon industry best practices, that reward participants for the achievement of specific, defined measures of outstanding performance and outcomes. Also, develop a financial model of the incentive plan costs over a wide range of potential outcomes.

6. **Long-term stakeholder plan:** Where appropriate, develop a long-term plan (or plans) that reflect and reward the creation of shareholder or long-term value. Such plans typically include granting guidelines for stock options, stock, or other equity instruments, or equity-like (*phantom*) plans, as appropriate. Often, this involves researching market stock option granting practices (e.g., How many shares? At what price are grants made? How do options vest?) as the basis for recommending stock option granting guidelines to the company and its employees/producers. If long-term plans entail cash awards, assess the cost of such awards over a wide range of outcomes and develop measures for making sensible long-term cash awards that can be adjusted to account for economic circumstances.

Even having set down these six steps, the plan will not work if it is not affordable to the firm or if it runs counter to the best interests of the firm's clients. For these reasons, any compensation plan must be accompanied by a study of how it fits into the overall strategic initiatives of the company. This should be done in concert with a cost-benefit analysis to ensure the affordability of the plan. Perhaps most important, conduct an impact study on how such a plan affects the firm's clients.

Some common mistakes made in compensation plan design involve a failure to consider the potential impact of a future economic downturn (with subsequent loss of firm revenue). With static plans (fixed salary plus bonuses), the costs can quickly spiral out of control, given less revenue to handle such expenses. Yet there may be solid reasons to employ a fixed component to a plan. It is important to structure plans to account for firm profitability in some meaningful way. A variable component is often paired with such profitability, as it can be built with exclusions in years where the firm experiences flat or negative revenue growth.

Another mistake is in promising too high a payout with assumptions on productivity that never materialize. It is far more difficult to negotiate down on compensation than up. Yet another mistake is to focus on new business production, leaving advisors with little motivation to service existing clients. This is where new business payouts are weighted heavier than existing AUM-related compensation. The opposite is equally egregious. This is where the compensation is based solely on servicing existing clients, which might be a disincentive to go out and find new clients.

The solution is to create a plan that delicately balances the new business needs of the firm with the proper servicing of existing clients, and to do so with an affordable program that motivates advisors (employees) to be more productive and engaged in firm goals. Thus, attempting to create a compensation plan without tying it in some meaningful way to the firm's strategic plans is clearly a mistake.

The biggest mistake of all is to assume that a compensation plan can and should be developed in a vacuum, without considering other business aspects that could be affected. As an example, a firm might choose to develop a compensation plan now, leaving the work of developing a business continuity plan (BCP) for later. Yet, the BCP might be constructed with dependencies on elements of the compensation plan or vice versa. Developing both as part of a comprehensive compensation/business continuity plan would avoid costly reworking of either plan at a later time.

In another example, consider the negative impact of developing a compensation plan that covers only a portion of the firm's employees/advisors. In this case, perhaps a firm has decided to implement a new compensation plan for producing advisors/reps while leaving intact the current compensation arrangements for other types of employees. With bonus plans and/or incentive programs limited to only part of the team, the result could be disenchanted other employees who feel alienated by the process.

This brings us to one final point about the development of compensation plans: They should be a collaborative effort that includes input from all affected members of the firm. You are much more likely to get buy-in from employees if they have at least some say in how this plan is developed.

You may choose to take this journey by yourself or with the help of a third-party consultant. But, ensure that whomever you work with has considerable experience in developing such plans. Paraphrasing the words of Gustave Flaubert, "The devil is in the details."

With consideration for all that has transpired in recent years, with extraordinary market volatility, mortgage and banking crises, client fears, and revenue challenges from declining assets under management, it may be hard to fathom the relative importance of employee policy manuals. However, the lack of employment policies or improperly prepared policies could be costing you more than you realize.

With financial advisory firms facing the prospect of declining profits, finding more efficient ways to manage a practice is a reasonable step for firm owners to take. One of the most fundamental steps in managing employees is in the establishment and enforcement of rules for the workplace; rules that govern what your employees can and cannot do. The value of establishing such rules is multifaceted. First, you can set standards of work performance and behavior for employees to follow. Second, you can establish those aspects of behavior that are deemed inappropriate for the workplace.

Standard provisions, such as work hours, holidays, company benefits, and so forth, can be enhanced to protect the firm from potential abuses by errant employees.

As an example, setting work hours is a standard provision. However, if you set work hours as 9 A.M. to 5 P.M. and then a salaried employee shows up consistently late for work and fails to make up the time, there might not be any repercussions for that employee unless there is a provision for negative consequences if the time is not made up in some other way (reduction of personal days or a cut in the next paycheck). An employee who is given 30 minutes for lunch but takes close to an hour is costing the firm money if that time is not made up. If a firm pays for eight hours of productivity (salary), it is reasonable for it to expect eight hours of productive work from the employee.

This may seem like nitpicking, but in tight budget times, multiplying the effect of similar abuses by employees over the course of an entire year could result in thousands of dollars spent on employee salaries that are not matched by an equivalent amount of productive work. Certainly, employee manuals are intended to do more than just enforce work standards. But, this is one example of how the lack of properly written policies could be costing your firm.

Another example is an Internet use policy. Many firms establish a policy prohibiting personal use of the Internet, particularly using company computers to visit questionable websites, download potentially harmful software, images, or other media, or visit chat rooms or use instant messaging. All of these activities could be harmful to the firm. Having questionable websites or images appear on a computer screen that could be viewed by others, especially clients, could open the firm up to potential lawsuits, sexual harassment claims, or worse. Having unauthorized software downloads could subject the firm to malicious software, Trojan viruses, or intrusive software intended to extract personally identifiable information. Even more, employees who spend time on these types of activities are stealing time away from their work activities for personal reasons. Ultimately, this costs the firm money.

Yet another example is a policy regarding personal cell phone use. One of the more difficult policies to enforce is a limitation or prohibition of the use of a cell phone during work hours. Younger employees grew up with cell phones and text messaging. For them, it is inconceivable to go through a day without access to one. Yet such use clearly interferes with an employee's office duties. Studies have shown that an interruption of an analytical task, however brief, could result in 25 minutes (on average) of an employee's time needed before that employee can mentally get back on task (University of California at Irvine Study, 2006). Given a personal text message that must be read and responded to (potentially another 2 minutes), one e-mail message could cost 27 minutes. Multiply this times four or five messages per day, times four employees, times 20 days of work per month, and you could be looking at over 2,000 hours per year lost. At $30 per hour, this could be costing the firm more than an employee's yearly salary in lost productivity. Yet, because the infraction is so sublime and the costs are not readily quantifiable, employers often don't recognize it for the huge expense that it is.

Annual vacation time, personal days, sick days, or other identified time that might be subject to compensation is another area for abuse. As an example, say an employee has banked 15 sick days and 21 vacation days because neither was used during a lengthy period of time on the job. The employee then decided to take all 36 days at the same time (because, in this example, the policy manual does not specifically prohibit this). At the conclusion of this time, the employee quits. The result is a substantial gap in productivity, not to mention the costs of hiring and training a new person to take over. Such a situation begs for a provision in the manual to cap banked days (or require they be used within a specified period of time). It also raises a question about how you time your paydays. Staggered paydays (the actual payday or deposit date of an ACH paycheck) can be set one week after the actual pay period to minimize sudden employee departures.

Many employers view the employee policy manual as defensive in nature. And this is true to an extent. Providing information relative to employment status, for instance, as regulated by the Fair Labor Standards Act (FLSA), or by state law, or as subsequently amended by either, is one way to ensure compliance with applicable laws and regulations. Indemnifying the firm against potential employee lawsuits, wrongful termination lawsuits, discrimination, unemployment compensation claims, or other lawsuits is certainly a defensive aspect of the manual. The FLSA, enacted in 1938 and amended many times since, sets minimum wage requirements, overtime pay, recordkeeping, and other standards for employment. (For a fact sheet on the FLSA as applicable to the financial services industry, visit www.dol.gov/esa/whd/regs/compliance/fairpay/fs17m_financial.pdf.)

HANDLING CONFIDENTIAL INFORMATION

Yet another important aspect of the employee manual involves the provisions for handling confidential client information. Employees should be held to a privacy standard and asked to sign a *nondisclosure/non-solicitation* type of agreement, even if they are not licensed individuals. This is because an employee could leave to join another firm and bring a prospect list of your current clients with her, unless the policy manual spells out the legal consequences of doing so.

However, the employee manual should not be just about potential negative aspects of work. The manual is an opportunity for the firm to paint a picture of the firm and what it is like to work there. This should include a mission/vision statement, a set of core beliefs related to the value of employees and the environment in which they perform best, and a statement on any changes in policy made with the latest version of the manual. It should also include work hours, breaks, how clients should be treated in communications, and what is expected of the employee with respect to working with others in the firm. The manual can outline all the benefits of working in the firm, such as retirement plans, medical, dental, life, disability, vacations, sick days, jury duty pay, and so on.

Truly inspired employee manuals weave the quality of the client experience into the manual to give employees, old and new, a perspective on the expectations of the firm with respect to how clients should be treated. If written in clear, unambiguous language, it is likely to be easier to comprehend and more efficient to administer. The most efficient manuals are those that accomplish all of the above while lifting the spirit of the employee rather than weighing it down with a list of negatives.

The employee manual, as important as it is, does not take the place of active management of your employees. In a profession fraught with increasing profit pressures, finding time to manage employees can be more than just a simple challenge for financial advisors. For some practitioners, management takes the form of damage control, rather than a well-thought-out proactive approach to the oversight of employees. At the other end of the spectrum, micromanagement can be found. Both of these approaches are usually inefficient and unprofitable and lead to further problems. One solution is to take a *systems approach* that is holistic in nature, offering efficient management techniques within an environment that fosters individual employee growth. To understand the application of such a solution, let us look at a couple of hypothetical examples.

TWO EXAMPLES

Example #1

In this first hypothetical example, we have J&J Financial Services, a full-service financial planning and asset management firm with two full-time employees and one part-time employee. John J., the principal, operates a Registered Investment Advisory (RIA) firm that is also affiliated with an independent broker/dealer (B/D). Owing to the dual nature of the business, the firm is subject to SEC compliance procedures along with FINRA and B/D compliance rules that have placed a great burden on employees from a paperwork perspective. To try to counter the enormous compliance demands, the firm has purchased scanning equipment and indexing software to convert all client files and other compliance-oriented files to electronic form, as much as possible. With a 10-year backlog of paper files to convert along with some 800 client files in multiple folders and in different locations, the unintended effect was to put an enormous additional workload on the employees to perform the file conversion while being expected to continue to keep up with their other daily duties. The file project was sprung on the employees with no advance warning (a common occurrence according to the employees) and with little or no training on the new scanning procedures. The result was uncontrolled chaos and employee resentment.

At this point, the principal, John, had to step in to perform damage control. Decisions had to be made to cut down on the workload for his employees—decisions that would likely cost the firm money and delay the process of conversion. Moreover, he had to deal with disgruntled employees. The irony is that all of this could have been easily avoided with a systematic approach to management of employees that involved more than the immediate needs of the firm (in other words, a holistic approach).

Example #2

In our second hypothetical example, we have Pro-mark Wealth Advisors; an RIA firm that has no FINRA registrations (independent). Pro-mark has eight employees and one principal, Markus L. Pro-mark does tax preparation work in addition to wealth management. The firm deals mainly with retired clients who have investable assets that exceed $1 million. Markus has a 10-minute egg-timer placed prominently on his desk. He explains that during the course of his daily activities, he turns the egg-timer. When it runs out, he gets up from his desk (interrupting whatever he is doing, including the possibility of a client appointment) to walk around to each of his employee's desks to see what they are working on. He sees this as a visible sign of his commitment to support his employees. The employees think he is an insufferable micromanager who is so paranoid that he cannot keep his hands off the wheel for an instant. The problem extends to more than employee dissatisfaction (which in this case results in a 50% annual employee turnover rate). Clients are allowed to see this going on, which negatively influences their level of confidence in the firm (and the likelihood of referrals). Micromanagement has also affected time management for Markus, the principal "rainmaker" for the firm. With such a demanding and detail-oriented schedule and virtually no task delegation skills, there is precious little time to generate new clients. The result is an inefficient and unprofitable firm.

THE HOLISTIC APPROACH

Both of the previous examples could be positively impacted using a holistic approach to management of employees. What is this holistic approach, and how can you integrate it into your firm? To answer that question, consider the chart in Figure 3.1.

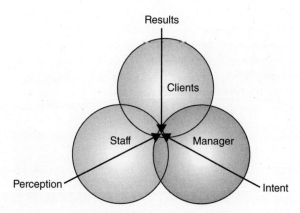

FIGURE 3.1 Holistic Communications Matrix
Source: ©Copyright 2006, David Lawrence and Associates.

The chart illustrates an important point about communications that relates to a holistic view of your practice. Enacting a decision in your practice without considering the effect it may have on others can have unintended negative impacts on your practice from a variety of perspectives. In the chart, your intent in communications must match the perception of those receiving the communication in order to achieve the desired result. Often, practitioners are in such a hurry to get the job done that they neglect to take the time to ensure that what they meant to say is what is actually heard. Thus, the first phase in developing a holistic management process is *communication*.

The second phase is to turn your employees into *stakeholders*. If they have a stake in the success of your practice, they are much more likely to support your decisions on the firm that could favorably affect them as well. Building stakeholder relationships with your employees based on trust can be a powerful way to increase the efficiency and profitability of your firm. This can be accomplished in a number of different ways, including tying compensation and bonuses to firm profitability.

The third phase is to develop an *employee management process* that is objective, fair, reasonable, and fully understood and agreed to by your employees. This is easier said than done. One way to approach such a process is to develop job outlines—detailed outlines of position responsibilities, expectations, and behaviors that are consistent with the overall vision, mission, and/or goals of the firm. Once developed, these can be dually used as a means of identifying and training employees and as a means of evaluating the performance of those same employees, using the same objective criteria described in the position outlines. The employee management process then becomes a three-step system as illustrated in Figure 3.2.

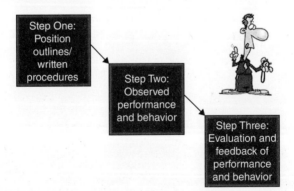

FIGURE 3.2   Objective Employee Management Process

By developing the position outlines as a minimum set of acceptable expectancies, you do not limit yourself to what you may ask of an employee. You merely set up a process to evaluate that employee on an objective (rather than subjective) basis.

Following these criteria, it is much easier and less risky to reduce the micromanager's stranglehold on the firm and to allow employees to take on additional responsibilities with less managerial oversight.

Workflow management should be fully integrated into this process (see Chapter 8 for details). Assigning tasks, being able to track task completion, both from an efficiency and proficiency standpoint, and effectively handling task delegation should be seamlessly wrapped into the employee management process, taking into account the motivations and skill sets of the employees measured against the needs of the firm. The results will undoubtedly speak for themselves in increased productivity and profitability along with greater client and employee satisfaction levels.

Employee management constitutes one of the great challenges in managing a financial practice. Even when things are going well, it can be a challenge to keep and motivate employees. Keeping high levels of productivity in an office can also be a challenge. So, when there is the possibility of an employee termination, for whatever reasons, it only adds to this challenge. How do you handle an employee transition, regardless of the circumstances?

To answer this question, first determine what sort of termination is looming. There are essentially two types: voluntary and involuntary. Under the voluntary category, this could be a mutual decision between you and the employee to part company, or it could mean that the employee has chosen to leave on his own. Either way, there is a procedure that should be followed.

Under the involuntary category, the procedure is similar to the voluntary one, but with some needed extra steps. Let's take a look at the voluntary procedure first.

You should consider developing an employment termination checklist. This would entail a number of items to be considered, such as company property to be returned (keys, laptops, handbooks, badges, parking passes, etc.). Also, there should be a list of computer-related issues to address, such as removing information from any home computer related to the company, locking access (remote or otherwise) to the office computers/servers, review and change of any/all passwords that apply, cancellation of the employee's e-mail account(s), and automatic notification to clients that the employee is no longer with the firm.

Other issues include a determination of any wages or other compensation that may be due and payable (vacation accrued, etc.), continuation of health insurance coverage (COBRA or otherwise), and other employee benefits that may apply. Removal of the employee's information from the company website, removal of the employee's voicemail message, and removal of the employee as a contact in press releases, and so on, are also necessary and should be on the checklist.

If the employee had a company-issued credit card or signature authority for any banking or credit accounts, this should be addressed as well. Security issues include the possibility of changing locks on doors and/or changing entry codes on keypad locks. Relocating petty cash or access to the company's checkbook may also be necessary. Don't forget to change passwords for online banking if applicable. The completed checklist should be placed in the employee's file.

While this seems like a lot to consider, it is only part of the steps needed to fully protect the firm. Some states have statutes that must be considered in employee termination cases. *Right-to-work* laws and *at-will* employment laws can have an impact on the viability and/or potential financial consequences of terminating an employee. For those states that have at-will employment laws, the definition of an employment relationship is one in which either party can break the relationship with no liability, provided there was no express contract for a definite term governing the employment relationship and that the employer does not belong to a collective bargaining group (i.e., has not recognized a union). Under this legal doctrine:

> [A]ny hiring is presumed to be "at will"; that is, the employer is free to discharge individuals "for good cause, or bad cause, or no cause at all," and the employee is equally free to quit, strike, or otherwise cease work.

Mark A. Rothstein, Andria S. Knapp, and Lance
Liebman, *Cases and Materials on Employment Law*
(New York: Foundation Press, 1987), 738.

Most U.S. states observe at-will employment. Consequently, there may be no legal consequences to terminating an employee for cause or no cause. However, there still may be financial consequences, particularly in the area of unemployment compensation and impact on the firm's federal and state unemployment tax rate. For this reason, it is critical for the firm to document the reasons for the termination in the event that it must defend its position in light of an unemployment claim.

The aforementioned checklist is part of this process of defending the firm. An additional step that is strongly encouraged is an exit interview in which the terms of the termination are fully discussed. The exit interview should contain the following sections:

Employee Name:

Termination Date:

Employee ID#:

Eligible for Rehire?

[   ] Yes

[   ] No

Job Title:

Job Code:

Reason for Termination:

Voluntary:

Involuntary:

[   ] Another Position

[   ] Attendance

[   ] Personal Reasons

[   ] Violation of Company Policy

[   ] Relocation

[   ] Layoff

[   ] Retirement

[   ] Reorganization

[   ] Return to School

[   ] Position Eliminated

[   ] Other

[   ] Other

Additionally, the exit interview form should contain sections that record the comments of the interviewer and a section for the departing employee to fill out, stating his or her side of the story along with a place for the person to sign, acknowledging that he or she understands the reasons. The purpose is to offer the opportunity for fair access to the employment record. The employee may feel unjustly terminated and, without being given the chance to state his or her side of the story, could walk away with a bad feeling about the company that could result in negative publicity or legal action for the firm. While it is likely with involuntary terminations that bad feelings will result, the purpose of the exit interview is to mitigate those feelings as much as possible and permit the employee to, at the very least, fully understand the circumstances surrounding the decision to terminate his or her employment.

In cases where the termination is due to circumstances outside of the employee's control (such as the elimination of a position), it may be prudent to offer help in the placement of that employee with another firm. This help may be predicated on the longevity of the employee with the firm and the applicability of that person's skill set to another firm's needs. At the very least, it constitutes a best-efforts attempt to help that should leave that departing employee with a better feeling about the termination.

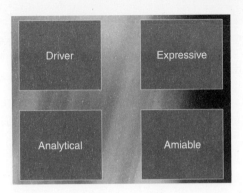

FIGURE 3.3   Social Styles

Certainly, the financial considerations are also a way to leave a departing employee with a more favorable impression. Calculating what is fair and just in compensating the terminated employee is a key issue. In cases where the termination is for cause, the financial compensation should be limited to what is actually owed to the employee (such as accrued vacation time, unpaid compensation, etc.). With the employee who is terminated due to other reasons (such as the position being eliminated), consideration should be made for some forward compensation in addition to the accrued benefits. This forward compensation may be calculated based on longevity (more than five years on the job qualifies for x weeks' severance, etc.). But, it is critical to pre-document this scale in an employment manual with all the qualifiers.

In the end, the goal of a termination is to leave the firm in a better place and to, as much as possible, leave the departing employee with a good feeling after the termination. Obviously, there are times when this may not be possible, but that is the goal. Fully documenting the reasons for termination and taking all the necessary steps can prevent future issues or security problems and protect the firm going forward.

Whether we are talking about hiring, managing, or terminating employees, communication is not a one-way street. Thus, leaders must not only understand the leadership communication styles, but also be able to respond to the social styles of the listener. Consider the chart shown in Figure 3.3.

Charts such as this have been written about for years (*Non-Manipulative Selling*, by Tony Alessandra, Phil Wexler, and Rick Barrea, Prentice Hall, 1987). Yet, on a day-to-day basis, it is often a neglected aspect of management communications. For example, a "driver" social style may work in communicating with an "amiable," but not necessarily with another driver. Thus, recognizing what social style the listener displays can help a leader adjust his or her style to effect better communication with those who are led.

THE RIGHT JOB DONE BY THE RIGHT PEOPLE

Clearly, one of the greatest challenges for financial advisors is managing time. Efficient use of time is often a confusing issue as there are many opportunities to misuse one's time. Yet, often it is the lack of sufficient time that leads to the greatest frustrations in a financial advisor's career.

As financial advisors spread themselves ever thinner, tackling from three to six different roles, on average, efficient time management becomes harder and harder to achieve. A new study by Mavenlink (www.mavenlink.com), for example, shows that one in four small business owners believe each productive hour in a day is worth upwards of $500. Yet, those same business owners are often seen doing tasks that could have been delegated to another employee at a far lower cost per hour. For financial advisors, such time-demanders could be tasks such as:

- Excessive and unprioritized e-mail reading
- Surfing the Internet
- Doing financial plan inputs
- Filling out forms
- Looking up data online

Other surveys have pointed to the increased burden placed on these advisors in recent years, including one by Sage Small Business that found small business owners are not only working harder than they were five years ago; they're also working longer hours. Another survey by Citibank found that owners are sacrificing their pay as well as family or vacation time, in addition to working longer hours.

These studies seem to confirm an earlier study by EfficientPractice.com as shown in Figure 3.4.

As can be seen from the figure, more than 50 percent of time in any given work day is eaten up by back office tasks. The irony of the graphic is the most valuable use of the financial advisor's time, generally regarded as face-to-face time with the client, represents the smallest percentage of overall time. Often, the reason why this is true is because of a lack of proper delegating. With efficient delegation techniques in place,

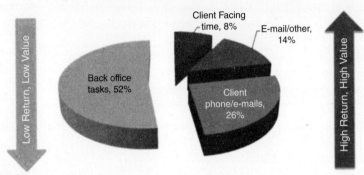

FIGURE 3.4   Time Allocation Study
Source: Based on EfficientPractice.com Survey ©2012

a firm could free up significant amounts of time, increase the capacity of the firm to accept new business (without necessarily having to hire more people or increase expenditures), and greatly increase the firm owner's personal time.

One way to get a handle on how your time is being used (or abused) is to keep track of what you do for a typical week. There are a number of ways to do this, from keeping a notebook to utilizing time-tracking software (some types are available for smartphones, for instance). The point is to be truthful and accurate in studying how you spend your time at work. The goal is to uncover things that you are doing that perhaps you should not be doing. Most of us are guilty of taking on tasks that could be handled by someone else.

Therefore, one of the most effective ways to manage a financial advisor's time is through the use of efficient delegating of tasks. As your business grows, you may find that in order to continue to move forward, you need to start handing over some of your daily to-dos to someone who can get the work done and free up your time for other, higher-level business activities.

But although it may be necessary, delegation can be a very difficult step for many financial advisors. This may be due in part to how they started in the profession, essentially doing it all themselves. With firm growth, this quickly becomes a roadblock to future success. Some of the hurdles advisors may have to jump in order to delegate efficiently include:

■ Feeling that they need to do everything themselves to have it done right

- Not having the time or desire to transfer the knowledge necessary to have someone else take over
- Being unable to find people they trust enough to delegate to

While these are all valid and significant hurdles, financial advisors can overcome all of their reservations by taking a well-planned and logical approach to delegation. There are five steps that should be considered:

1. **Identify those tasks that should be delegated:** In every financial practice, there are some things that can be delegated and others that should not. For example, you should probably avoid delegating tasks that require a higher level of knowledge and/or experience than is possessed by those who might be delegated to. And it is really important to fully and clearly define the task that is being delegated.
2. **Make sure you are delegating a task to the right person:** Developing position outlines for your staff that define their roles in the firm is a good first step to identifying what tasks should be undertaken and by whom.
3. **Provide clear documentation and instructions:** For repetitive tasks, this constitutes a workflow management system or developed task sets. With clear instructions, the employee has a much better chance of completing the task(s) correctly, efficiently, and on time.
4. **Develop workflow tracking systems:** Rather than micromanaging your employees, use workflow management tools (many are already embedded in client relationship management software) to quickly view what work is in progress in your office.
5. **Provide feedback:** It is just as important to let your employees know when they are doing the tasks correctly as when they are falling short of expectations. The process of feedback can also uncover gaps in the workflow process and provide clues to improve the system.

By providing your employees with responsibility assigned within the limits of accountability, you create an opportunity for those employees to grow and be more motivated to do good work.

Some financial advisors have paired this technique with a compensation program with individual and team bonuses, based on specific, objective performance criteria. These bonus structures may be developed and paid more frequently (such as quarterly) instead of the old traditional annual bonuses paid out at year-end. Tying bonuses to performance criteria, such as on-time completion of tasks, accuracy, and/or error-free work, can definitely tie the firm goals to those of the employees.

Replacing micromanagement with effective workflow management systems has the effect of erasing distrust and increasing overall performance standards. And, most important, the financial advisor can free up significant amounts of time that can be redirected to client-facing activities or simply more personal time.

SUMMARY

Chapter 3 studies how financial advisory firms should approach the management of human resources and communication skills. The chapter offers guidelines on how to hire the right people, and what sort of steps should be involved in the search for new employees, including background information. Additionally, advice is offered on how to conduct potential employee interviews and how to analyze the information obtained to identify and properly hire the right person.

Managing employees has to take on more than just hiring the right people. Advisors need to understand how to support those employees, train them effectively, and oversee their efforts without appearing to micromanage. There is a host of tools and techniques offered to assist in this endeavor.

Employee manuals, which should be a set of guidelines for the employee to understand and agree to, can provide a number of essential rules for employee activities and behavior on the job. Such aspects as the handling of confidential client information (for instance), a critical feature of any financial advisor's practice, must be clearly outlined so that employees understand their responsibilities.

One key aspect of the employee management process is compensation. Developing a compensation plan that embraces and rewards high levels of efficiency and productivity is essential to achieving greater net profitability for the firm.

The chapter offers two examples of employee management issues confronted by real advisory firms (though the names were changed to protect the privacy of these firms), followed by a discussion on the holistic approach to employee management.

Additionally, the chapter explores the right job done by the right people. It looks at what happens when, for example, a senior advisor is doing work that is better suited to one of his or her employees. Not only does it frustrate the employees, but it is a time-demander on that senior advisor, when his or her time would be better spent on higher-level tasks such as meeting with clients and prospects. Efficiency is damaged when such activities are present. But, for some advisors, who started in the business as sole practitioners and were forced to do it all, it is difficult to give up those tasks. Learning how to delegate within the limits of responsibility and accountability with managerial tools that can observe employee performance without the need for constant oversight can lead to much higher levels of efficiency and firm success.

Technology Efficiency

CHAPTER 4

Client Relationship Management

Technology has revolutionized the financial services profession. It has given us the ability to analyze investment trends, make trades, produce reports, and track client portfolios, to name a few. However, in the rush to take advantage of technology, many practitioners have ignored the potential benefits of efficient use of technological systems.

To offer a definition, technical systems efficiency is where your technical systems, such as computers, printers, telecommunications, software, and so on, all work in smooth harmony with each other, sharing information seamlessly and transparently with the client. Yet, many financial practitioners work with a hodgepodge of equipment and software, purchased at different times, without consideration as to how well that technology will integrate with existing equipment and software. Often, this leads to substantial challenges in trying to make systems talk to each other. Perhaps the first step in dealing with this issue would be to make an inventory of equipment and software. Then, determine to what extent these various inventory items can be made to work together.

LEVERAGING TECHNOLOGY

One fundamental question with technical systems is to understand fully how you wish to use it versus how it is actually capable of being used. You cannot ask technological machines to perform tasks for which they were not designed (in most cases). But, in many cases, financial advisors are underutilizing their technology, rather than overutilizing it.

Therefore, it may be possible to increase the use and/or leverage of technology in a practice by better understanding it. This knowledge should encompass more than just individual pieces of equipment. A holistic approach is generally recommended, where hardware, software, technological systems, and procedures for using these systems are all taken as a whole with the goal of finding ways to integrate those various pieces of the puzzle.

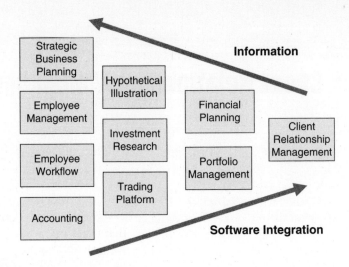

FIGURE 4.1   Technology Puzzle

As an example, let us take a look at typical software solutions found in a financial advisor's practice.

The chart in Figure 4.1 illustrates a hierarchy of information read, interpreted, analyzed, or otherwise utilized by the financial advisor and/or his or her staff. The painful truth of this chart lies in the knowledge that all information should be, but seldom is, shared across these divergent software platforms. When the same data must be typed in over and over again, there can be a substantial cost in staff time and frustration.

An example of inefficiency with respect to software might be the financial advisor who uses Microsoft Outlook for client contact management, but uses some other client relationship management software for historical and personal information storage. Microsoft Outlook is not a true relational database. A relational database ties historical records with contact records and offers the ability to search the database using a variety of flexible criteria. Reports can be generated that can be customized to fit the needs of the practice. Outlook does none of this. It is an excellent e-mail program with some contact record capabilities. Nevertheless, if what the practice needs is a full relational database, Outlook is not going to satisfy the need (although Outlook 2007 is significantly improved in this area). Alternatives that are frequently chosen include Goldmine, Junxure-I, ProTracker, and ACT! for Advisors. These four are all relational databases. Junxure-I and ProTracker coordinate with Outlook (offering the ability to continue to use Outlook as a main e-mail portal). Goldmine is popular with financial practices that work with insurance products. Junxure is popular with financial planning and asset management firms and ACT! is popular with everyone else. The advantage of using a program such as Junxure or ProTracker is that it is preconfigured for use in a financial practice. Goldmine and ACT! may require substantial customization to work the way your practice might need.

As for coordination with other programs, the point in using a relational database is to have access to information easily and quickly and to be able to migrate that information to other programs without the need (and the time involved) to retype the information. As much as possible, efficiency can be achieved in typing in information only once. On this score, Outlook offers export capabilities to Excel spreadsheets. But, most relational database programs offer the same feature. The advantage is that other programs, such as financial planning, portfolio management, illustration software, risk management software, asset allocation software, and Monte Carlo simulation software, may accept comma-delimited format imports of client data. By being able to export out of your customer relationship management (CRM) program into an Excel spreadsheet in a comma-delimited format and then being able to import that same data into another software program, the time savings is enormous compared with having to retype all that information over and over again.

Financial advisory firms position themselves for long-term profitability when they embrace the importance of client relationships. Effective relationships help firms find new clients, build client loyalty, and increase the value clients receive from them. Therefore, strengthening client relationships should be not only a goal of financial advisors, but also a top priority. Surprisingly, few actually systematically map out what that relationship should be, much less build an efficient client relationship model.

The importance of building a model lies in the ability to consistently apply the steps in the model across all aspects of a financial advisor's practice. If an advisor devises such a model and then fails to share it with his or her employees (for instance), then the model is effectively rendered useless.

Customer Relationship Management

Much can be learned by studying what the big boys do. Large corporations have long embraced a comprehensive approach to client (customer) relationships. Client relationship management (CRM) typically spans all aspects of a corporate business structure from front office to back office and records direct and indirect interactions with clients to build a powerful database that can be used to better manage those same relationships. Key data can be analyzed to plan target-marketing campaigns, build effective business strategies, and weigh the effectiveness of current services based on a variety of criteria and metrics.

Though most financial advisory firms lack the financial resources to match the CRM initiatives of the large corporations, there are still many lessons to be learned and much of what they do can be emulated (albeit on a smaller scale).

Technology considerations should include a well-rounded CRM software program that can capture all relevant information on client data, interactions, and historical records. The database should be capable of collecting information about each client and their interactions with the firm, such as appointments, financial data (investments, transactions, risk considerations, estate issues, etc.), personal data (including subtleties such as client interests, children's activities, etc.), client requests, survey responses, and even client use and participation in client offerings (such as client appreciation events, website content usage, etc.).

This data can and should be analyzed to better understand the needs and wants of a firm's clients from a variety of perspectives. Survey data can often uncover weak areas in client service offerings or overdone service offerings. (i.e., too much paperwork sent to the client).

Client relationship management software is generally regarded as a must-have solution for financial advisors. In a perfect world, CRM software not only can warehouse client data and historical information, but can perform necessary tasks related to the client experience. Yet despite sales claims from some vendors, CRM software is not a one-size-fits-all solution. That being said, there are a few that may come close. But, to find the right solution for your financial practice, you need to do your homework.

Here are five steps that can lead you to the right solution:

1. **Determine your needs:** You will need to take a hard look at your financial practice operations and list the functions that can make your firm perform more efficiently. Your needs in the areas of client information storage, data aggregation and/or collation, employee task assignment, scheduling, and automated workflow management are a few of the many functions that should be considered in this process. Often, firms want to filter these types of decisions based on the central theme of "How is this going to benefit my client?" rather than just considering the impact on the firm and its employees.
2. **Determine your budget:** Are there budgetary constraints that may affect the decision-making process? As an example, a firm with a small client

base may find it difficult to afford a top-end solution, particularly if the solution includes functions that may not be fully utilized by the firm.

3. **Consider your options:** In the world of CRM software providers, there are many types of solutions. You may wish to consider whether you should purchase off-the-shelf software, basic CRM software, a full-featured product, or an integrated solution. Even within each of these options, there are several choices. Things to consider are the features, functionality, integration with other softwares you may use, and presentation of information in a way that fits your style of practice. With apologies to the many software providers, here are a few choices to consider:

   a. **Off-the-shelf choices:** Act! (Including Act! for Advisors, www .act4advisors.com), Goldmine (including the Breaking Away Version, http://www.ticomix.com/Customer-Relationship-Management/ BreakingAway), and so forth. While these are popular choices, limitations include potential inability to link client data from other sources, limited workflow management features, and so on. Benefits may include lower onetime cost (with the potential cost of upgrades later).

   b. **Web-based off-the-shelf:** Salesforce CRM (www.salesforce.com/crm) and Microsoft Dynamics CRM (www.crm.dynamics.com). While both of these solutions are feature-rich and popular, they may require substantial customization to fit the way a financial practice operates. With per-user subscription pricing, costs can quickly add up.

   c. **Financial advisor configured solutions:** In this category, there are several choices, among them Redtail Technology (www .redtailtechnology.com), a popular web-based solution that has great features, including a flexible workflow management and task assignment system, multiple integrations with outside data providers and softwares, and competitive pricing. Junxure (www .junxure.com) is a server-based solution with highly customizable features and a feature-laden interface that is regarded by many experts as high-end. One surprising entry in this category is Advisors Assistant (www.advisorsassistant.com). It is surprising in that, although it has been around for a while many advisors have dismissed it based on its prior functionality. However, Advisors Assistant has increased its functionality, including a new, updated interface, easier navigation, and improved workflow management, and it contains broker/dealer-appreciated features such as master accounts and assigned databases, which are desperately needed by many B/Ds needing supervisory-type configurations. It is also useful with multi-advisor offices needing segregated databases with some centralized functionality (such as shared staff access to client information, etc.). It also has advanced capabilities to auto-capture insurance valuation data, critically missing in other solutions.

d. **Integrated/holistic solutions:** Two notable choices in this category include Interactive Advisory Software (www.IASSoftware.com) and eMoney Advisor (www.emoneyadvisor.com). Both of these are outstanding solutions for what they do. However, consideration should be made for whether all of the pieces of the solution match what the firm is looking for. In both cases, though, they seem willing to work with outside integrations. IAS is a holistic solution, a true shared database with multiple modules that can tap into that database and perform complementary functions. eMoney offers integration of data across all functions, sometimes referred to as a *silo system*. Both offer outstanding client portals.

4. **Review the institutional issues:** Depending on how you are set up, you may be a broker/dealer–affiliated firm, an independent RIA, or other type of firm. If you work with an institution, custodian, or B/D, chances are there may be choices available to you at discounted prices that could affect the purchase decision. In cases where a CRM is available through an institution at an attractive price, but the functional aspects of the software do not exactly match what you are looking for, it may be wise to see if a customized version can be created to better fit your situation and needs. In many cases, these institutional choices could be preconfigured with data integrations to make the task of automating the data aggregation/collation that much easier. They may also have been configured to share data with other programs offered by the institution that you need (i.e., financial planning software, portfolio management software, etc.).

5. **Perform a return-on-investment (ROI) calculation:** This type of calculation can go a long way to convince a financial advisor of the wisdom of the particular choice being considered. In this calculation, you need to consider all of the costs associated with the purchase. That should include both the hard-dollar and the soft-dollar costs/benefits. Some of the line items that should be considered in this process include:

a. Costs:
   i. **Purchase price** (subscription cost): Hard-dollar cost
   ii. **Installation cost** (some software companies offer data migration services at no cost, others charge fees): Hard-dollar cost
   iii. **Customization cost** (using a third-party provider to customize the database or build add-ons): Hard-dollar cost

      iv. **Employee conversion costs** (to spend time converting/verifying data to the new software): Hard-dollar cost

      v. **Employee aggravation:** Soft-dollar cost (hard to measure)

  b. Benefits:

      i. **Increased efficiency:** Expressed in employee hourly costs saved—hard-dollar benefit

      ii. **Increased profits:** Potentially lowering operational costs can extend net profitability, even in cases where no additional gross revenue is realized—hard-dollar benefit

      iii. **Increased capacity:** The ability of the firm to take on more clients, without necessarily hiring more employees, increasing office space, or purchasing additional equipment—hard-dollar benefit

      iv. **Increased practice value:** Extending what a firm can do, expanding its reach, its potential, and its services, most often results in a higher practice value—hard-dollar benefit

      v. **Creating a more harmonious work environment:** Soft-dollar benefit

Another key consideration in purchasing and, especially, replacing a CRM software that may have been used for a period of time by employees, is the potential for pushback by those same employees. Therefore, a key piece of advice to heed would be to include your staff in the decision-making process. Performing the ROI calculations might be helpful in this process as you could document the actual benefit to the employees (as well as clients) of utilizing the new CRM solution.

Data Gathering and Analysis

Website usage data can uncover unused features of a website and/or heavy usage of a particular area of the website that might be expanded to meet a need. Ignoring such data could be wasteful and costly and lead to client dissatisfaction. Most website hosting services offer usage data, often broken down into specific areas of the website, to provide useful tools in changing, upgrading, improving, and deleting content.

Environmental scans provide needed additional information on a financial advisory firm's service offerings relative to a variety of factors, including such things as your client's opinions, competitors' services, employee perspectives, and market area demographics. As part of the environmental scan you may wish to consider two ideas for information gathering: (1) client focus groups—this would be a onetime session with a broad selection of client groups to discuss the relative merits of current service offerings (everything from quarterly reports, website features, and client meeting content to client communications, etc.); and (2) advisory council (group)—this would be a select group of clients asked to serve on such a council to meet periodically (perhaps once or twice a year) and to be available via e-mail for specific issue discussions relevant to the firm and its clients. As this group could be recognized on a letterhead, website, or other medium, it could be presented as an appointment of some distinction (attractive to some clients). And it provides a valuable, ongoing resource to bounce ideas off of.

Ultimately, the purpose of gathering such data for analysis is to build a client relationship model that matches the needs, wants, and expectations of the client. Elements to consider in constructing a relationship model should include:

- **Letters:** Birthday cards, anniversary cards, Thanksgiving cards, correspondence, confirmations, and so on.
- **E-mails:** Announcements, information (nonpersonal), invitations, alerts, requests (such as to contact the office for an appointment, confirmations, etc.).
- **Phone calls:** Incoming (live person), outgoing (appointment setups, etc.).
- **Face-to-face meetings:** Quarterly meetings, informal get-togethers, and so on.
- **Web 2.0 functions:** When the client visits your website, it pushes customized content (such as personalized greetings, user-selectable page content features, menu item choices, etc.).

Letters and e-mails can be a very powerful way to strengthen relationships with clients by assuring that follow-up communications are timely and reassuring. As an example, a client hands you a check to be invested into a group of investments, per a previous discussion. If an advisor collects the check and then does nothing, chances are the custodian would send out a confirmation to the client. However, this could take several days.

In the meantime, the client is left to worry about whether the money was invested timely and correctly. By immediately sending out a confirmation e-mail or letter (acknowledgment), the client is reassured that the investments are being handled professionally and in a timely manner. This is true for most client- and/or advisor-initiated requests. It is simply a best practice to keep the client informed. With advanced client relationship management software, the task is easy and quick. With most software of this type, it can be as simple as a single button click to load an e-mail (or letter) template with personalized client information and send it.

Here is a partial list of these types of communications:

- Transaction acknowledgments
- Rebalancing notifications
- Appointment reminders
- Beneficiary changes
- Ownership changes
- New client welcome
- Meeting notes/confirmation of decisions

Web 2.0 offers the promise of revolutionizing client relationships in a profound and compelling way. By being able to customize content to each client or visitor to your website, you can effectively personalize the look and feel of the website to suit the needs of individual clients. As an example of such technology, consider Amazon (www.amazon.com). Amazon creates a customized page (see Figure 4.2) with suggestions for additional purchases when someone views a particular product.

While it is unlikely that a financial advisory firm would tie such Web 2.0 content pushing to individual products, a subtle use of this technology might be in recognizing which pages of your website have been visited by a particular client and suggesting a conversation with an advisor on that topic or area of interest, creating an RSS feed suggestion (*really simple syndication—* a method to push news, information, etc. based on content selection) or a specific invitation to meet with an advisor.

This kind of personalized content impacts client relationships through the realization by the clients that their situation and needs are being addressed on multiple levels, providing several choices on where and how they wish to receive information and communications. It also distances the firm from a one-size-fits-all approach, by creating compelling personalized visuals that differentiate the firm from its competition.

The financial advisory profession was built on the foundation of phone calls and face-to-face communications. Even though the profession has moved in the direction of technology, it would be foolish to ignore the power of the spoken word. Ultimately, clients want and need to hear from you, not a recording.

The desired end result of the client relationship model should be a symbiotic relationship between the advisor and the client. This may be characterized by the recognition of mutual goals, the client to reach certain financial goals and the advisor to fully understand the client's financial situation and needs relative to those goals. It can also be characterized by the mutual trust and respect the client and advisor have for each other.

Best Value

Buy **Overcoming the Five Dysfunctions of a Team: A Field Guide for Leaders, Managers, and Facilitators** and get **The Five Dysfunctions of a Team: A Leadership Fable** at an additional 5% off Amazon.com's everyday low price.

Buy Together Today: $32.12

[Add both to Cart]

Customers Who Bought This Item Also Bought

Overcoming the Five Dysfunctions of a Team: A Field Guide for... by Patrick M. Lencioni
★★★★★ (23) $16.47

Death by Meeting: A Leadership Fable...About Solving the Most... by Patrick M. Lencioni
★★★★★ (78) $16.47

The Four Obsessions of an Extraordinary Executive: A Leadershi... by Patrick M. Lencioni
★★★★★ (49) $16.47

Silos, Politics and Turf Wars: A Leadership Fable About Destro... by Patrick M. Lencioni
★★★★☆ (40) $16.47

The Five Temptations of a CEO: A Leadership Fable by Patrick M. Lencioni
★★★★☆ (65) $16.52

Related Items

The Five Dysfunctions of a Team: Participant Workbook
~~$40.00~~ $38.04

Overcoming the Five Dysfunctions of a Team: A Field Guide for Leaders, Managers, and Facilitators
~~$24.95~~ $16.47

FIGURE 4.2 Amazon Customized Page

SUMMARY

One of the key pieces of the technology puzzle is, or should be, the client relationship management software. It is intended to be the focal point for all client communication, records, workflows, and scheduling. Thus, selecting the right CRM for your practice is an extremely important decision. Many firms make that choice based on the recommendations of others, or based on the latest hot product on the market. This chapter points out why making the decision on this basis is fundamentally flawed, as it ignores the specific needs of the firm. Yes, there are new, fancy softwares being introduced in the financial services profession every year. But the choice for your firm should be based on several factors, outlined herein. One of the key factors to consider is whether the software you are looking at is actually compatible with and can share data with the other software programs that the firm has already invested in.

Many advisors have expressed concerns about the security of software programs that are offered on the *cloud*. Sometimes referred to as *software as a service* (SaaS), in the early adoption of these platforms there were valid concerns about security. However, with the SEC and FINRA weighing in on acceptable standards for information security, software makers have made great strides in securing data with higher encryption standards and auto-resets of passwords, along with platform-level intrusion detection systems. The issue about security has largely been addressed effectively.

Chapter 4 also addresses the issue of client data gathering and analysis. There are a number of resources available to help financial advisors collect information in an effort to better know the clients. On a larger scale, advisors use such techniques as environmental scans, focus groups, surveys, and other means to better understand client needs on a practice level. These techniques can additionally provide clues to the financial practice's differentiation strategy. In other words, by studying your clients on a global level, you may uncover common issues that could reveal a unique differentiation (or unique skill set of the firm) that can then be used in marketing. It can also lead to a narrower focus, which can improve the efficiency of a firm that previously was attempting to be all things to all people.

Other Software Issues

People are often fond of gadgets. Gadgets can make life easier and more fun. The popularity of the iPhone, for instance, is proof of how a cleverly marketed gadget can capture the imagination of the consumer. In the financial services world, there are numerous gadgets that may be used by financial advisors. From desktop tools to software to peripheral equipment, there is a variety of such items from which advisors can choose. The challenge is finding those tools that can actually improve the efficiency of the financial advisor instead of creating an unnecessary distraction.

EVERNOTE

One tool that could be an inexpensive way to boost collaboration among staff in an office is Evernote (www.evernote.com). Evernote is a great note-taking tool that is free, unless you upgrade to the Premium edition. You're always moving; your notes should be, too. With Evernote, your memories are on every computer, phone, and device you use. Save entire webpages to your Evernote account with their nifty browser extensions. You get the whole page: text, images, and links. Share your notes and collaborate on projects with colleagues and others on a permissioned basis.

With Evernote, all of your notes, web clips, files, and images are made available on every device and computer you use. Additionally, Evernote integrates with Microsoft Outlook and permits you to capture all or just part of an e-mail with the click of a button for saving and sharing. Also, Evernote can capture voice notes for later playback, for those times when typing on a computer, laptop, or phone device is just not convenient.

As a collaboration tool, Evernote can provide a communication-sharing venue for quick notes, ideas, concepts, and images that can be shared with others for discussion or collaboration. Attempting to text instructions to staff while on the go can be time consuming and frustrating, depending on the device used. With Evernote, details can be quickly and efficiently disseminated to staff.

DIGITAL NOTE-TAKING TOOLS

One of the more difficult aspects of client meetings for advisors is trying to listen to what the client is saying while attempting to take accurate notes. There are two tools that could prove useful in this endeavor. The first is using a digital recording device that is compatible with voice recognition software. Typically, these two items are bundled. Nuance Dragon Naturally Speaking (www.nuance.com) offers such a bundle. Its latest software edition boasts no training required for up to 99 percent levels of accuracy.

However, it should be pointed out that, if you already own or have recently upgraded your operating system to Windows 7, there is voice recognition software already included in the Windows 7 software that rivals the accuracy of Dragon. As an example, you might decide to use a laptop in a client meeting; it could be configured to capture and show the text conversion during the meeting. Uses of recording devices in client meetings are subject to privacy rules and may be prohibited by compliance rules imposed by your broker/dealer. Check for such rules prior to use, and in every case the client's permission should be obtained.

The second tool, in this regard, is a digital pen. Digital pens can capture whatever you write and transform it into text in a computer. There are two models worth checking out. One is Livescribe (www.livescribe.com). The Livescribe Echo SmartPen offers the ability to write notes and then transform them into text on a computer. It also has an audio capability so that you may be able to not only write your notes, but capture the audio for later conversion to text. Livescribe can come bundled with Evernote and is fully compatible with Evernote (mentioned earlier). Livescribe Echo requires the use of a special grid paper.

For this reason, you might wish to check out another digital pen from Logipen (www.logipen.com). Logipen advertises that it can be used with any paper, by clipping a device onto the pad of paper you might be using, instead of the use of grid paper. Logipen does not have the audio capability, but at half the price of Livescribe, is certainly worth checking out.

Yet another set of choices for note taking that have gained in popularity are mobile dictation services. There are at least two that focus on the financial services profession. One worth checking out is Copytalk (www.copytalk.com), and the other is Mobile Assistant (www.mobileassistant.us). Both offer an efficient solution for capturing notes. Also both have arranged integrations with select client relationship management software (CRM) solutions that permit the direct deposit of transcribed notes into the CRM program. Both offer apps for mobile devices that permit direct dictation from that device.

Copytalk touts its call center operations, which centralize its dictation personnel in secure U.S. locations with onsite supervisory oversight. For those advisors who have concerns about the security of their client's data, this focus on security is a definite plus. Copytalk also offers a flexible set of delivery options, either e-mailed directly to you or entered directly into your CRM software. Copytalk has been chosen by a number of larger broker/dealers for its compliance compatibility.

Mobile Assistant touts its unlimited dictation time (with some exceptions) and additionally offers the ability to dictate directly into a form created by the user (e.g., client follow-up letter template, etc.). It also offers an iPhone application for mobile dictation purposes. While Mobile Assistant uses outsourced transcribers, it points to its platform as HIPAA and Gramm-Leach-Bliley compliant. For those advisors looking for a flexible solution (dictation time and/or choice of delivery), Mobile Assistant is worth checking out.

The real advantage of using a mobile dictation service is not necessarily the features, security, price, or compliance, but the ease of use. Unlike using voice recognition software where it could take up to 30 days of continuous use to become proficient, mobile dictation services take almost no time to get up to speed. And, unlike traditional note-taking, with either you or a staff member copying the notes into a client record, editing those notes, and so on, mobile transcription services do the work for you. The accuracy of the transcriptions is likely to be higher, and, because these services are dedicated to that one task, the speed of delivery is likely to be faster and less distracting than if you or a member of your staff undertook that same task. Doing a simple cost comparison, for what you might pay each month for mobile transcription services that could result in dozens of transcriptions, you might end up paying the same amount for two hours of staff time. Mobile transcription is faster, easier to get up to speed and use, more efficient, and ultimately way less expensive than if you undertook the same tasks in-house.

TABLETS AND STORAGE SOLUTIONS

More and more, advisors are using the iPad tablet computer as an efficiency tool. Paired with the iPhone, it can be helpful as a data collector and display device. As a processing tool, it is limited in its ability to compete with a full-featured laptop. And, until recently, the storage capacity of the iPad was a serious impediment. However, Apple has now introduced the iCloud. iCloud is more than a hard drive in the sky. It makes it quick and effortless to access just about everything on the devices you use every day. iCloud automatically and securely stores content so it's always available to your iPhone, iPad, iPod touch, Mac, or PC. It gives you access to your documents, music, applications, latest photos, and more from whichever device you happen to be using. And it keeps your e-mail, contacts, and calendars up to date across all your devices. No syncing is required. No management is required. In fact, no anything is required. iCloud does it all for you. When you sign up for iCloud, you automatically get 5 GB of free storage. And that's plenty of room, because of the way iCloud stores your content.

If you do not like or want to go the Apple route, no worries, as both Microsoft and Google offer competing products (that have been around longer, by the way). Microsoft offers Office Live (with SkyDrive), and Google Docs was the first of the online storage solutions.

Whether you choose the Apple product or others, the concept is the same. Documents and information are stored online for easy retrieval and sharing. Other pure storage solutions that auto-sync with various devices are such notables as Dropbox, NetDocuments, and Sugar Sync. Again, though, these solutions may be subject to compliance rules and/or regulatory restrictions.

With any of the aforementioned devices, gadgets, tools, or software, a pivotal question should be asked before going out and purchasing or obtaining the item: How is this solution going to benefit my client and my practice? Often, simply buying the latest fad and then trying to figure out a way to fit it into the operations of a firm is counterproductive and can lead to inefficiency (or a waste of valuable time). First, identify the need, and then investigate your options. In the end, you may stand a better chance of making efficient use of the product selected.

With increased regulation and, in some instances, overlapping regulations that constrain business and add to increased workload, storage needs, and added staff training, never has there been a greater need to employ the technologies that surround electronic document management than now. Sometimes referred to as *electronic content management* (ECM), such systems take on a much larger role in a financial advisory practice when all potential aspects of the system are employed.

Most firms look at document management as filing. Whether it be a paper-based file system or electronic files, the firm may have set up informal procedures for handling documents within the firm. One key aspect of a properly designed ECM is whether formal workflow procedures and controls have been integrated with the system. With some firms, this means tying the ECM to a database (client relationship management software, for instance). For others, it means setting up a standalone indexing system based loosely on a folder tree such as what you would find on a computer's operating system. Without specific, strict controls, the risk with informal systems is that documents would be misfiled or, worse, that employees unfamiliar with the folder tree would simply create new folders for items that should have been placed elsewhere. This makes document retrieval difficult and frustrating, to say the least.

A common mistake that is made by some firms is to use a system that saves documents in PDF format instead of a more secure format (such as TIFF). This raises questions about the possibility of documents having been altered after the fact and exposes the firm to possible risk associated with noncompliance with federal regulations. While some scanner manufacturers have addressed this issue with post-imprint symbols and other coding mechanisms to ensure authenticity, there is still some lingering doubt about the security of the original document.

While it may be tough to justify any additional expense, the simple truth is that by employing a highly efficient document management system, costs can go down over time—way down. This softens the blow of any upfront expense and fully justifies the time commitment necessary to implement such systems.

If you are associated with a broker/dealer, chances are the B/D is already offering some level of document management (i.e., forms capture, pre-fillable forms, outsourced electronic storage, etc.). If not, there is a host of available systems that can transform your financial practice into a highly efficient operation, simply by going paperless.

The SEC and FINRA have both ruled on the acceptability of paperless storage, retrieval, and recovery. They have even ruled on the acceptability of electronic signatures (with specific guidelines). Among the rules that must be observed, a proper document management process should include provisions for establishing, maintaining, and demonstrating compliance with regulations such as SEC and FINRA rules, Sarbanes-Oxley, and the USA PATRIOT Act. There should also be a way to provide an audit trail.

So, what is stopping you? Chances are two things, cost and the knowledge necessary to get the job done right. Consider the expense and use of a typical system such as Laserfiche Avante (www.laserfiche.com). The Avante system was designed to be scalable and affordable by setting pricing based on usage. A typical install for an office with, say, four employees who are using the system might cost initially around $4,000. While this sounds like a lot of money, consider what such a system could do in shaving staff time and increasing productivity and profitability. With such a system, there would be a much faster document storage and retrieval process. Because the office could go paperless, there is a substantial savings in square footage of needed office space, and the reduction of staff time could equal the salary of another employee. So, you may wish to ask yourself, would I be willing to spend $4,000 to save upwards of $40,000? Consider that the annual renewal costs are much less, but the savings continue.

At the Laserfiche Institute Conference, held in Los Angeles on January 12–14, 2009, company founder and president, Nien Ling Wacker, expressed her goal of making the company the sweetheart of information technology (IT) by introducing firms to a new line of products such as their workflow and easy integration with Microsoft products such as SharePoint—as she put it in her keynote address: "expanding sales and systems from document management to business process management." This message seemed to resonate throughout the conference, attended by over 1,000 people.

Most financial advisors are only aware of Laserfiche as a provider of document management solutions for the financial advisory profession. However, it was clear from comments made at the conference that Laserfiche has penetrated virtually every level of society, including such clients as the Mexican Immigration Service, the country of Uganda, and the U.S. Congress, all of whom use Laserfiche's technology.

And while Laserfiche is a strong presence in this market space, Xerox has also made inroads with its DocuShare Express product (www.docushare .com). DocuShare Express is also a robust system for electronic content management (ECM). Offered to small and medium businesses (SMBs), DocuShare provides a turnkey solution for scanning and document storage and retrieval. DocuShare Express developed the ability for employees to view and share documents online through a web browser as a key collaboration component and function of its system. And, as Xerox is a scanner manufacturer as well, there is tight integration with the scanning equipment if the Xerox scanners are chosen. There is also the ability to migrate into a more robust enterprise-level system later, should the firm grow.

Both of these systems are Sarbanes-Oxley compliant, Gramm-Leach-Bliley compliant, and SEC Rule 17a-4 compliant. One reason for this is the file types created and stored. Most use a TIFF image, generally regarded as an unalterable form for electronic storage.

Yet another piece of the document management puzzle is the documents themselves. Many broker/dealers provide PDF versions of forms, some pre-fillable. B/Ds may also require secure transmittal of forms through proprietary systems owned or operated by the B/D. While this may provide some efficiencies, for those firms that use forms not provided by the B/D, there may be a need to locate a reliable source. For this need, there are at least two reliable sources available, LaserApps (www.laserapps.com) and QuikForms (www.quikforms.com). Though these types of firms typically offer thousands of forms for download, advisors typically only use a few forms. It would be wise to ensure that the forms you need are actually located in their database before signing up. Also, you may discover a willingness to add a form, if it is not part of their inventory. You can also create your own pre-fillable forms in cases where they are not available elsewhere. For this, you need Adobe Acrobat (www.adobe.com) standard or professional version. There is a much-overlooked feature in Acrobat that permits you to take a PDF and create pre-fillable form fields. As you may only need to do this to a few forms, it could save hours of staff labor.

However you choose to create documents, using a comprehensive document management system with automated workflow features could significantly increase the efficiency and profitability of your practice.

REBALANCING SOFTWARE

Another software issue that has proven to be frustrating for financial advisors is rebalancing software. Efficient rebalancing requires software that can be an expensive tool, depending on the needs and complexities of the financial practice. One of the ironies of passive asset allocation strategies is that there are times when they are not so passive. If an advisor's asset allocation models are customized to fit the needs of a particular client, there is a significant investment of time in setting up, monitoring, and potentially rebalancing the client's portfolio.

Some advisors have set up their rebalancing triggers based on an arbitrary percent-out-of-mix flag. Let's say that you use 1 percent as the benchmark. When the portfolio skews more than 1 percent away from the original percentages identified in the asset allocation for each asset class, rebalancing would occur. This sort of tight rebalance trigger could create a lot of work for the advisor and/or the staff responsible for the trades to keep up with rebalancing. With a wider percent, say 25–30 percent variance selected, it could open up the portfolio to greater risk.

With a largely flat market, maybe the percent is not so important. But, when the market is experiencing higher volatility, having a wider percent variable could inadvertently cause buys/sells that are counter to the client's best interests. So, some advisors have installed timing triggers to account for potential speed bumps in a particular asset class's performance. As an example, let us say we had 15 percent of a portfolio in small-cap growth and the asset class grows out of mix. With a timing trigger, this would establish a buffer where if it falls and then rises within the timeframe, no trade would have occurred and no harm done.

However, if we do this, do we not now have to install both down-market timing triggers and up-market timing triggers? And, conceivably, they would be different. With a down-market trigger, it might be wise to have a shorter time period to mitigate the potential downside risk. In an up market the timing trigger could be somewhat longer.

Other advisors have embarked on calendar rebalancing, preferring to rebalance perhaps once each year toward the end of the year. This technique would seem to ignore market conditions and simply be reactive to what is the condition of the allocation at the point of rebalancing (time of year, conditions of the market at that time, etc.).

There could be other triggers involved. There could be general economic triggers, market condition triggers, asset class freeze triggers (under special conditions), and others. This creates an active trading strategy and not a passive strategic asset allocation. Sometimes referred to as *dynamic asset allocation*, the Society of Asset Allocators and Fund Timers (SAAFTI) was founded upon this principle. Renamed the National Association of Active Investment Managers in 2004 (NAAIM) (visit: www.naaim.org), the organization is dedicated to the idea that active management of investment accounts can mitigate downside risk and improve risk-adjusted returns over those of the static allocation technique.

Critics of active timing strategies point out that research has shown timing accounts for only around 6 percent of a portfolio's overall performance. They also point out that 91 percent of a portfolio's performance is achieved through the power of the mix of assets by class. Furthermore, critics argue that the transactional costs and potential tax liabilities make this an unattractive alternative to clients.

Whether you embrace traditional strategic allocations techniques or venture into the world of actively trading in and out of asset classes within an allocation, there is still a lot of work to do to manage the portfolio and optimize the returns for clients, given their risk constraints.

The question is what methods are available to optimize portfolios and rebalance those same portfolios. Some advisors choose to use a makeshift Excel spreadsheet, while others prefer a developed software platform. With Excel, it is possible to construct a fairly sophisticated asset-rebalancing spreadsheet with several triggering mechanisms. You can even use conditional formatting to reveal by color when a particular asset is, for example, a buy, hold, or sell position based on those triggers. If you are building this yourself, high degrees of knowledge in developing Excel spreadsheets that use web queries and other data-linking techniques are needed. The advantage of using Excel is its flexibility; the disadvantage is the time it takes to develop what you want and keep it compliant. With developed software packages, the likelihood is that they use approved methods, and the time taken in this instance is to learn the software, not develop it. A disadvantage might be that you would have to accept whatever rebalancing tools are included in the package (i.e., less flexibility, maybe).

Whatever your choice, there are a few questions you may want to ask:

1. Does your broker/dealer offer a rebalancing tool?
2. Does your method tie trades from your B/D or clearing platform to your software?
3. Can you do batch rebalancing?
4. Can you set upper and lower limits on certain asset classes such as bonds?
5. Can you set locks to exclude certain asset classes from rebalancing?
6. Can you set minimum transaction amounts?
7. Can you set a specific dollar or percent cash buffer?

You may also want to explore what other tools are included in a particular software solution such as asset allocation proposals and Monte Carlo tools.

One software program that seems to fit the bill is an offering from ASI Advisor Software (www.advisorsoftware.com). Advisor Software, Inc. recently unveiled the latest version of its ASI Portfolio Rebalancing Solution®, which enables financial services enterprises to streamline portfolio rebalancing. This new release delivers a competitive advantage for financial services companies, further automating time-intensive rebalancing processes and boosting advisor efficiency, according to the company. With this version, advisors can rebalance more than 100 accounts simultaneously. Additionally, key features include cash buffers, locking enhancements, and tolerance bands. The company has provided TDAmeritrade with its portfolio-rebalancing tool, among other well-known providers.

Another software program worth looking at is BridgePortfolio (www.bridgeportfolio.com), which offers a comprehensive back-office outsourcing solution that includes asset allocation, portfolio management, and reporting. With automated features for data capture and delivery through a web portal to and from clients, such a solution could potentially save thousands each year in operational costs.

On the expensive side, iRebal (www.irebal.com) stands out as a high-end, feature-rich software. At $50,000 a year, this might sound expensive, but when compared to the internal costs of providing similar services, if done by advisors and staff at this level (up to 1 billion AUM, 1,000 clients, etc.), the cost for a fairly large firm could easily reach two to three times this amount or more.

A couple of others to look at are Tamarac Advisor (www.tamaracinc.com) and eAllocator (www.eallocator.net). Both of these have interesting features, global rebalancing capabilities and the ability to rebalance individual portfolios or families of portfolios. Yet another, more cost-effective solution is Total Rebalance Expert (www.trxpert.com).

If you are intent on doing it yourself, automation features are a way to speed up the process of producing rebalanced portfolios. Having systematic ways to create the rebalance and effect the trades necessary to accomplish it is key to making the process move quickly, efficiently, and with no errors.

Fixing trade errors can be both time consuming and expensive. So getting it right the first time is necessary and cost efficient. Training staff to perform the tasks necessary to rebalance a client's portfolio should include written procedures they can easily follow. Having a decision-tree type of flowchart in addition to the written steps can help train employees who are more visually oriented.

Last, but certainly not least, is the need to communicate rebalancing with your clients. If your portfolio management software permits, having the ability to batch-upload reports and notices and announcements to your clients via a secure, encrypted lockbox feature on your website gives the client quicker access to the information while saving your firm money in ink, printing, paper, and mailing costs. Though not all your clients may feel comfortable with this, if 60 percent or more were receptive to information delivery through a web portal, the savings would be significant, and your office could operate more efficiently.

SUMMARY

People love gadgets. Gadgets can be fun, and sometimes they can be useful. But, as with all forms of technology, gadgets can also be a distraction and in some cases actually limit what you can do. As an example, consider the Apple iPhone. The iPhone has been a phenomenal sales success for Apple because it frequently introduces new models with additional functionality (or gadgetry) that catches the imagination of the consumer. One problem with this is how an advisory firm can best utilize that functionality and to what extent it might be limited by it. With respect to the iPhone and iPad tablet, one major issue is the ability (or lack thereof) to share data seamlessly with other systems, particularly non-Apple systems such as Microsoft Office softwares (very commonly used in financial advisory firms).

In most cases, the owner of the Apple product has to perform a two-step manual process to share the data. The two-step process may involve third-party software that can receive the info from the Apple product and then translate it for use in the Microsoft product. Additionally, being able to print from Apple products is possible, but not necessarily easy. For this reason, it is recommended for business use that advisors consider other options, such as the Windows phone and Microsoft-friendly tablet computers, where those types of devices are needed.

Chapter 5 also looks at more efficient ways to take notes, using such tools as Evernote and other solutions. Using mobile transcription solutions, though not necessarily high-tech, can be a more efficient way to record notes, pass instructions to staff, and/or capture thoughts following a client meeting.

The chapter concludes with some thoughts on rebalancing software, often one of the most time-demanding, labor-intensive aspects of a financial advisory practice's work. Yet, it is also a critical task, if the firm manages money on behalf of its clients. So, not only finding the most efficient solution is important, but finding one that works the way the firm needs it to is critical. Having said this, rebalancing software is one of the most expensive solutions out there. Yet, there are clear choices, some more expensive than others. With those choices are a number of varying levels of functionality. It is important for advisory firms to find the solution that works for them, not just the fanciest (or priciest) version.

Finding more efficient ways to deliver detailed investment performance information to your clients is another aspect of efficiency. Some of the softwares offer a client portal with a secure encrypted lockbox for client use. Being able to deliver this investment data accurately, cost efficiently, and securely to your client not only can save the firm time and money, it can also strengthen the client relationship for those clients who elect to use the lockbox feature.

CHAPTER 6

Systems Integration

One of the goals of efficiency is to reduce or eliminate repetitive tasks wherever possible. With software, this generally means the reduction of keystrokes and the repetitive typing of the same information into divergent applications. Such items as birthdates, Social Security numbers, addresses, phone numbers, and so on form the bulk of wasted staff time when employees are asked to type this same information over and over again. A database, particularly a relational database such as a client relationship management (CRM) software, is ideally suited to warehouse such data for use outside of its own functionality. However, all too often, one software program does not necessarily talk to another.

SOFTWARE INTEGRATION AND COMMUNICATION

How softwares talk to one another is through an *application programming interface* (API). The API is a language and message format used by an application program to communicate with the operating system or some other control program such as a database management system (DBMS) or communications protocol. APIs are implemented by writing software code that provides the linkage to the required other application. The API can be configured to map data fields from one program into corresponding fields of another such as in the case of a CRM program linking its data to a financial planning software. This type of linkage is typically done throughout the software industry. And, while the concept to the end-user appears simple, it is actually a complicated process that could involve thousands of lines of code and potentially expose a software's unique programming to another company (competitor). For this reason, software companies have been reluctant to embrace deals involving APIs.

In recent years, cooperation among software manufacturers has changed this line of thinking to some extent. Projects such as Your Silver Bullet (YSL) (www.yoursilverbullet.net), Schwab's Intelligent Integration, and TDAmeritrade's VEO project have encouraged software makers to share integration. And while the list at YSB is impressive, the integration is not universal. In other words, not all member companies are willing to fully integrate with all other members. Acceptance, though, is growing, especially in these tough economic times when companies recognize that to survive they must find ways to collaborate with peer companies.

Clearly, one of the advantages of selecting individual software packages that integrate with others is the flexibility in choices and use. With the use of a CRM package such as Junxure (www.gowithcrm.com), ProTracker (www.protracker.com), Redtail (www.redtailtechnologies.com), and others comes the ability to choose which one of them fits the way you run your practice and match it up with other software that you prefer to use, such as MoneyGuidePro (www.moneyguidepro.com), Naviplan (www.EISI.com), Money Tree (www.moneytree.com), and others. One of the drawbacks to the use of divergent companies is cost. Generally speaking, unless there is a discount offering associated with a group of softwares, the costs can start to add up, particularly with subscription software. Among the software offerings out there, one of the most costly tends to be broker-independent portfolio management software (iRebal, BridgePortfolio and Tamarac to name a few). Many of these programs are highly complex, sophisticated trading, rebalancing, and analysis platforms that must tie in to custodian servers and produce accurate reporting. For this, the costs understandably tend to rise, but not necessarily in every case.

This concept of integration has given rise to a new breed of software platforms, referred to as *integrated solutions*. The advantage of such platforms is that all components of the offering are able to seamlessly share data and coexist together on the same desktop. This affords the end-user the luxury of having one program up and able to quickly access all areas of the financial practice operations, from client contact data to portfolio management to financial and estate planning.

One offering in particular has generated some renewed interest with the recent release of its rebalancing module. That offering is Interactive Advisory Software (IAS) Solution 360° (www.iassoftware.com). Priced well below its contemporary competitors, the module (which must be purchased with the IAS portfolio management module) allows you to rebalance portfolios against a user-defined target model allocation. The tool automatically generates the most tax-efficient and lowest-cost transactions to accomplish the rebalancing goal. Among other things, leveraging this optimized rebalancing enables you to:

- Combine qualified and nonqualified accounts together in the same portfolio and rebalance accordingly.
- Lower back-office labor costs.

- Accelerate growth by attracting higher-end clients.
- Review and edit before the export file is sent to custodians for execution.
- Increase returns for clients.

The advantage of using an integrated software product suite such as IAS is the use of one database. But more than that, the tools, such as portfolio management, rebalancing, CRM, and financial planning, are all integrated through workflow features that permit highly efficient task completion with a minimum of keystrokes.

Despite its all-in-one approach, one surprising integration deal recently announced by IAS is a collaboration with Money Guide Pro. While such an integration might seem odd, given that IAS has its own financial planning module, the concept is to offer an integration with a goals-based planning platform that could complement its cash-flow-based module, which extends the reach of the platform and offers greater flexibility to the end-user.

Another integrated platform is eMoney Advisor (www.emoneyadvisor .com). With its similar-sounding 360° Pro product, it offers a comprehensive planning center with 11 modules covering virtually every aspect of a client's financial situation and needs. Additionally, it offers account aggregation, an online storage vault, mobile access, customized reporting capabilities, and alliance partnerships to permit collaboration with other trusted advisors such as attorneys and accountants.

Additionally, eMoney offers a goal-based platform called eMoney 360°. This version focuses on specific financial analysis that is modular and presentation oriented. With 11 standalone modules that can be utilized individually or consecutively, the platform provides readymade presentations that can be customized or added to on-the-fly.

eMoney offers yet another product called eMoney Everywhere. It connects the user to Microsoft Outlook, Redtail CRM, an iPhone 3G, Microsoft Excel, and BlackBerry for mobile accessibility that extends the efficiency of the financial advisor by permitting access to data and information virtually anywhere.

A third player in the software integration space is Advisor's Assistant (www.climark.com). Advisor's Assistant offers a powerful client management platform with investment and insurance tracking capabilities. Its portfolio management features appear to be limited, but they have developed alliances with AdvisoryWorld, Money Tree, LaserApps, Quikforms, and Morningstar to name a few. The platform has extensive daily download capabilities and additionally can download security prices and index values through an alliance with SunGard (for an additional monthly subscription fee). There does not appear to be a rebalancing feature or tax-efficient trading capabilities at this time. But Advisor's Assistant is a strong player in the client contact and marketing area along with insurance management tools often missing in other companies' products.

One fear of advisors has been that using one of these types of integrated platforms is limiting, in that the user would be restricted to only the tools provided by that company. But, as these products have grown and evolved, it has become apparent that outside integrations and alliances can greatly extend these platforms and offer the promise of additional choices and flexibility with the end result of a more efficient financial advisory practice.

PROTECTING CLIENT DATA

In this age of malicious software embedded in websites and spam e-mail, e-mail phishing, identity theft, electronic eavesdropping, computer viruses, and other means of stealing information, it would seem obvious to most financial advisors that taking steps to protect client and firm data would be warranted. Yet many firms still do not take these threats seriously, leaving information openly accessible to anyone who happens to wander by.

Let's take one case in point. An advisor welcomes clients into his office for a meeting, rather than a conference room. On his desk is piled a bunch of client files, including files of clients other than those seated in front of him. He steps out of the room for a moment to retrieve some papers, and the client glances at the files spread out on the desk. While this may seem to be an entirely innocent situation, it points out the vulnerability of financial advisors who are simply too busy to notice such details. Most of us trust that our clients are honest. But, under Regulation S-P of the Gramm-Leach-Bliley Act, the requirements are oblivious to the "honesty of a snooping person."

As required by the Gramm-Leach-Bliley Act, Regulation S-P (www.sec .gov/rules/final/34-42974.htm#P458_181230) generally requires every broker/ dealer, investment company, and investment adviser to:

- Provide each of its customers with a notice of its privacy policies and practices at the time of establishing the customer relationship (the initial notice) and annually thereafter (the annual notice).
- Provide each of its consumers (who have not yet become customers) with an initial notice before disclosing nonpublic personal information about that consumer to a nonaffiliated third party.
- Refrain from sharing nonpublic personal information about a consumer with a nonaffiliated third party unless the institution has provided the consumer with an initial notice and an additional notice describing that practice and the consumer's right to prevent it (the opt-out notice).

■ Adopt policies and procedures reasonably designed to (a) ensure the security and confidentiality of customer records and information; (b) protect against any anticipated threats or hazards to the security or integrity of customer records and information; and (c) protect against unauthorized access to or use of customer records or information that could result in substantial harm or inconvenience to any customer.

Therefore, taking reasonable steps to protect private information is clearly mandated by federal regulations and is simply a good practice to pursue. This raises the question, though, as to what the reasonable steps should be. One recent example involved a firm that has a large office with a separate file room. Though the file room is lockable, it is never locked because the building's cleaning crew needs access to empty trash and clean floors. The individual file cabinets chosen for this particular office are not individually lockable (though they could be adapted). It probably does not matter anyway, as several files were found lying around on work counters in the room. In other offices of this firm, client files were strewn on desks and even stacked on the floor. These were referred to as *working files*. Though these offices were able to be locked, the cleaning crew, building maintenance, and even (potentially) former employees have keys. The office has not been rekeyed in years. You might be thinking that this is an extreme example, but it is not. This is typical for offices visited by this consultant over the years.

This example points out one reasonable step, to protect client files by putting them away at the end of each day in a secure, locked environment inaccessible by unauthorized personnel. (Having electronic files—paperless solutions—increases security of this information and reduces or eliminates the problem of open files lying around.)

Another recent example involved firm information, in this case a company business Visa credit card account used for firm purchases. This card was frequently used for purchases made by the office manager (items such as office supplies, etc.). Rather than bother the owner of the firm with a request for the card number, expiration date, and security code, the office manager wrote this information down on a Post-It note and stuck it in an open drawer. This sort of method is an open invitation to anyone who has access to the office to steal that information. Though such credit card purchases, if illegal, can usually be reversed, it is the aggravation and time wasted in correcting a situation that eats into the financial advisory firm's profits. (See *Financial Advisor*, March 2008, for an article by David Drucker on identity theft.)

A third example involves the storage of user IDs and passwords to secure websites where client information can be found. Many firms simply write these down on a piece of paper or store it in a Microsoft Word

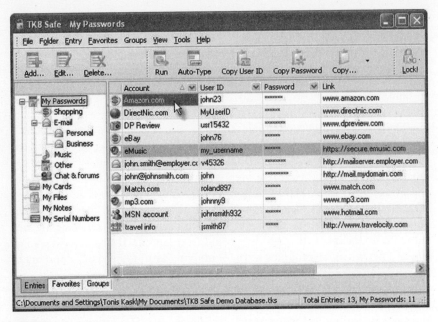

FIGURE 6.1   TK8 Safe

document. Access is sometimes difficult as the list may not be in alphabetical order. And leaving such a list out in the open (in one case, the list was tacked on a corkboard in the workroom of an office) invites unauthorized access and potential theft of client financial information.

These last two examples could be solved by using a secure, encrypted, and password-protected password storage software program. Such programs can store not only user IDs and passwords, but credit card information, protected files, and other information. There are many of these types of software solutions out there. One in particular that has two versions, a standard and a professional version that can be used in a networked environment with multiple users and varying access levels, is TK8 Safe (www .tk8.com), shown in Figure 6.1. TK8 Safe can do all of the above as well as auto linking to a site and has autotype features to make logging in fast and easy.

Firms should be careful to ensure that employees only use this type of software for firm-related business. Staff members who would be tempted to add their own bank accounts, credit cards, or website logins could open up the firm to risk, especially in the event of an SEC/FINRA-type audit. But, at $19.95 for a personal version of the software, employees may wish to consider purchasing this for home use.

One final example involves the security of e-mail communications. Much has been written about this subject. Yet, little is done to protect client information inside unencrypted e-mails. As an example, a financial advisor might e-mail one of his clients with an attachment showing the client's net worth, list of assets, and so forth. This type of e-mail is highly vulnerable. If you work with a broker/dealer, chances are there is an e-mail solution already in place and available for use that has security features. If you are an independent advisor, it may be up to you to install a system to protect your firm and your client's private information. Encrypting e-mails is somewhat unwieldy as it requires the recipient to have the key to unencrypt the message. If you use MS Outlook as your e-mail portal, for example, you would need to send a certificate file (.cer file) to the recipient, who then must add this to your contact record in their version of Outlook in order to see the messages that follow. For elderly clients or those unfamiliar with the Internet and e-mailing, this could be cumbersome to say the least. The workaround is to avoid sending personal client data via e-mail or to separate the data into several e-mails. Another choice is to add a secure lockbox (or vault) to your website and upload such documents there for client viewing. This method ensures encryption and password security. Most website providers for financial advisors provide lockbox or vault technology (e.g., www.advisorsquare .com, www.lightport.com, www.advisorsites.com, www.advisorwebsite.com, and www.emeraldconnect.com).

Your choices for information security should reflect your need to protect your firm's information as well as your clients' in a secure and efficient manner.

SUMMARY

Being able to share data across a variety of different softwares can be a tremendous time and money saver for a financial advisory firm. This chapter reviews ways in which this can be done. There have been a number of industry initiatives to facilitate software integration, including the Silver Bullet project, Schwab's Intelligent Integration, and TDAmeritrade's VEO project. Of the three, as of this writing, TDA's efforts have yielded more wide-ranging results. However, there is reason to understand all of those programs so that you can choose what best matches up with the collection of software that your firm employs.

There are also other ways to share data, and these concepts are explored as well in this chapter. Among the other ideas is utilizing an integrated solution, such as Interactive Advisory Software's platform of software (all sharing one database) or eMoney Advisor's platform that does the same. Both of these solutions have reached out to other softwares to be more flexible in their data integrations.

Even client relationship management software has gotten into this trend, with softwares such as Advisors Assistant and Redtail Technology opening the door to potential data integration with several other platforms.

However, despite all the choices, a chief concern has to be protecting client data, and this chapter addresses this concern. Several examples of potentially dangerous practices are illustrated along with suggestions on how a firm can protect such information through the use of encryption and password protection in a secure environment.

It is not enough to simply employ heightened security measures; these measures should be clearly communicated to clients. Your choices for information security should reflect your need to protect your firm's information as well as your client's in a secure and efficient manner.

Three

Process Efficiency

CHAPTER 7

Building Procedures

It may be no surprise that written policies and procedures would be linked in some way to profit. What is surprising is how few financial advisors actually take the time to write them. For some, it may seem redundant to create a set of manuals if they already have similar types of written materials provided by their broker/dealer. So, to be fair, let's differentiate between broker/dealer–type policies and procedures and those that should be created separately by the financial advisor. And, while we are at it, perhaps we should also explore the reasons behind such an exercise.

Generally speaking, policies and procedures that are developed by broker/dealers facilitate the processing of paperwork and/or transactions, ensure appropriate compliance requirements, and protect the broker/dealer. Following such procedures generally also protect the financial advisor. However, policies and procedures that relate specifically to the day-to-day operation of a financial practice are most always left to the financial advisor to develop or customize to his or her needs. So, to understand how to develop such things, it is critical to identify what it is about your practice that needs a written policy or procedure.

Starting with policies, some of the easiest to identify are those associated with employees. An employee manual (or guide) can set out the rules of behavior and actions, identify inappropriate actions, and spell out remedies. It can also provide details on employee benefits, vacations, sick time, and policies regarding such things as jury duty, family medical leave, sexual harassment, discrimination in the workplace, and so on. In short, the employee manual can serve as a guide to the employees, new and old, on what they need to know to work in your office environment. Items such as client relationship policies and office atmosphere issues where it relates to the client experience should be in the employee manual, but often are neglected.

Additionally, it may be a good idea to include a legal agreement that covers such things as non-compete/non-solicitation of clients, nondisclosure of information rules, and so on. Even if an employee is a non-licensed assistant, it is still a good idea to have such a document signed by that employee.

Check with your broker/dealer and/or seek legal advice before preparing such a document.

Another document that can be associated with an employee manual is a job description. This is not a one-page summary of duties, but a detailed line-by-line description of every expectation, activity, and responsibility for that specific employee position with accountability factors built in (how you intend to hold the employee accountable for those responsibilities, etc.). Writing job descriptions can be tricky. While you would want to be as detailed as needed, you may also want to leave room for additional tasks that may be assigned that fall outside the list. Otherwise, the employee could legitimately refuse to perform a particular task simply because it was "not on the list."

Closely related to the job description but far more time consuming to write are task-oriented procedures. Several advisors have mentioned that employees are reluctant to assist in the assembly of procedures manuals because they view the manual as a threat to their job security. One point to consider is the need to protect the vital functions of your practice versus one or more employees retaining control over tasks that cannot be replicated by others. The fact remains that if an employee is sick or quits, your practice could be in real trouble if that employee, for instance, was the only one who knew the procedures associated with trades (or the operation of a software platform that manages portfolios). Yes, you can call the software company or your broker/dealer or whomever to help. But, how much time and money is lost while all this is going on?

The key to maintaining up-to-date procedures manuals is not to make employees obsolete, but to allow any employee to be able to perform the functions of another employee (or, for that matter, the financial advisor) in a pinch. Such publications also make training new employees a snap. Task by task, they need only refer to the associated manual to know the step-by-step instructions on how to complete that task. You might consider suggesting to employees (who might otherwise be reluctant to assist you in preparing manuals) that merely having the manuals on hand makes these employees more valuable to you as they can step into anyone's role when needed.

What sort of procedures might be best suited to having a manual? Tasks associated with software such as client relationship management, asset (portfolio) management, trading platforms, illustration software, financial planning, asset allocation, and portfolio analysis are a few. It may be that the financial advisor performs certain higher-level tasks in these software packages, but uses an employee to perform initial data entry. Whatever the case, having written procedures in place makes your practice much more efficient and less prone to downtime.

You may also wish to fully document the paper trail; that is, record all the procedures required to submit documents, information, suitability requirements, applications, and so on that comprise the flow of business through your office. Some advisors prefer to draw out a flowchart that depicts each step in the workflow process. This is a good idea, but it should be accompanied by detailed written procedures on each step in the process.

Other procedures, such as phone etiquette, file preparation and handling, mail handling, compliance recordkeeping, and so on, may be grouped into a single "office procedures" handbook. Some advisors prefer to include these procedures in the employee manual. Be aware, though, that your broker/dealer may impose certain requirements with respect to separate record-keeping for compliance purposes.

There are a number of software products available to help you with the process of writing and maintaining office policies and procedures. One set of products from CCH/KnowledgePoint (www.knowledgepoint.com) addresses employee job descriptions, policy manuals, people management, and performance evaluations at a reasonable cost. Another product, from TemplateZone (www.templatezone.com), offers an office policy manual software package among other business software packages. Even Microsoft can help, offering literally dozens of free templates for policies and procedures on their main Office website (www.office.microsoft.com); click on templates!

If you look long and hard enough, you can find thousands of products and written guides to help you write policies and procedures. But, sooner and later, you are going to have to sit down and actually write them. So, before beginning this, you may want to ask yourself how this relates to efficiency and profit. The answer lies in understanding how systems can make the flow of business and accomplishment of tasks easier, faster, and more effective. By writing procedures, you get a first-hand look at how efficient (or inefficient) those existing procedures are. The exercise of writing the procedures can reveal ways to trim the process, refine your workflow systems, and make things work better in your practice. Freeing up your time and that of your employees can save you money. It can allow your practice to handle more clients, process more business, improve client relations, and increase employee satisfaction merely by going through the development of written policies and procedures. Let's look at a specific example.

FINANCIAL PLAN PRODUCTION PROCEDURE

Some practitioners might argue that the financial planning process is anything but efficient. This perception may be due in part to the way in which financial advisors choose to assemble financial plans. That perception leads to the question, "Is there a better way?" The answer may lie in how you want your financial plan to look once it's assembled.

In conversations with financial practitioners across the country, many have described an assembly process that uses a number of diverse elements. Many seem to feel that no one software program is capable of containing all the elements needed to produce the plan they want to present to their clients. Therefore, advisors often use a number of different programs to fill in the gaps or strengthen the overall presentation.

Use of unrelated programs that do not necessarily share data poses its own set of challenges. Often, information has to be typed into different programs over and over again. The eventual output from various sources may have the wrong pagination, contain different fonts and type sizes, and even look different owing to page design differences (headers, footers, auto-spacing, etc.).

The result is often a mishmash of software outputs jammed together in a three-ring binder and declared a financial plan. Though some might suggest that a financial plan doesn't have to be pretty, experts suggest that a document that is produced with a consistent look, such as typeface, headers, footers, colors, spacing, consecutive pagination, and so on, is more likely to be completely read and understood than a document that is not consistent in style and appearance. The fact remains that assembling a document can be a time-consuming task when working with diverse, unrelated software outputs.

Software manufacturers have not lost sight of this. Many now offer comprehensive solutions to financial planning production and are beginning to recognize the need to be able to share data from outside software products. And, with the trend toward web-based financial planning software solutions, the flexibility and ease of use can only get better over time. A couple of popular choices in this category are MoneyGuidePro (MGP) (www.moneyguidepro.com) and Naviplan (Zywave) (www.zywave.com/).

MoneyGuidePro offers unique collaboration features with its latest version (v. 6.0) that allows the planner to share whatever level of detail or access is needed with either a co-worker or with the client. The output design has been enhanced and shifted to landscape printing to be more visually appealing. MGP prints to an Adobe .pdf format. In describing MGP's ability to import information from a variety of sources, Robert Curtis, chief executive officer, mentioned that "the emphasis is on getting asset-level data." To that end, the company has forged data integration deals that integrate on a platform level. Their partnership with Investigo (www.investigo.net) is an example of this platform-level thinking. The end result is being able to share data across a platform that integrates client relationship management, portfolio management, and financial planning.

Naviplan Central offers a variety of levels of planning, based on the amount of specificity of details you might wish to share with the client. Each level is capable of building on the others, meaning that if you chose to produce a level-one plan now and upgrade the client to a level-two later, you could seamlessly integrate the data from the level-one plan without the necessity of reentering all the information. Their new Financial Assessment tool offers the opportunity to produce a quick look at such goals as retirement, education, major purchase, and/or life insurance for clients in about 10 minutes. Naviplan also offers collaboration features similar to MoneyGuidePro and offers workflow reports to simplify supervision of employees or collaboration partners. Naviplan's document output can be directed to an Adobe Acrobat .pdf format or to a Microsoft Word document.

Other, similar products include Advice America (http://advisorvision .adviceamerica.com/), and Interactive Advisory Solutions (IAS) (www .IASSoftware.com), though both offer features such as client relationship management and/or portfolio management components similar to the Investigo platform.

What if you are not using one of the previously mentioned software products and would still like to find ways to integrate outside sources into a consistent document? Depending on your chosen financial planning software, it still may be possible to create the desired end result. To begin, you will need a common assembly point. This could be Adobe Acrobat (www.adobe.com) or Microsoft Word (www.microsoft.com), depending on the structure of your software and how it chooses to print out documents. Most programs allow you to print to a specific printer and offer the ability to choose that printer. This gives you the opportunity to select a .pdf print driver as your chosen printer. Once selected, the document actually prints to a file with the .pdf extension. It is recommended that you own Adobe Acrobat 7.0 Professional for this purpose. Or, owing to copyright expirations, you can now choose a less expensive alternative such as pdf995 (www.pdf995.com). With Adobe Acrobat Pro 10.0+ or the Suite version of pdf995, you can then assemble a document from a variety of different outputs, creating a common look and feel to the document. Combining different .pdf files into a common document is a snap inside Adobe Acrobat 10.0. With the Professional Edition, you can even move pictures, graphs, and text or edit directly in the document(s). Using Microsoft Word as your document assembler is equally easy, using familiar cut-and-paste routines. And, Microsoft Word allows you to choose to paste into the document using destination formatting, which eliminates a step in formatting text.

However, there may be times when you only need to incorporate a single element such as a graph or table from a program into your plan. Or you may have encountered an information source that does not permit you to print to a pdf driver. If that is the case, there is a nifty little tool out there just for you, and the good news is it's free. It is called Screen Hunter (www. wisdom-soft.com), and it is a screen capture utility. (The paid version contains editing features not found in the free version.) With this little tool, you can snatch a small part of anything displayed on your screen and paste it into your assembled document. The quality of the captured image is remarkably good.

With practice, these document assembly techniques can greatly speed up and enhance the overall process of producing a financial plan document. Advanced techniques could include writing macro commands to automate the most common assembly tasks in an effort to increase the speed and efficiency of the overall financial plan production process.

FLOWCHARTS

There is also something to be said of flowcharting. Flowcharts can greatly enhance a procedures manual and also address a unique learning issue. Some employees learn better visually than by reading a bunch of words. So, incorporating a flowchart into a procedures manual can have the effect of accelerating the learning of new employees or employees new to a process. Figure 7.1 is an example of a client induction process.

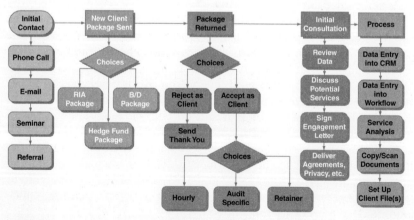

FIGURE 7.1 Sample Client Induction Process

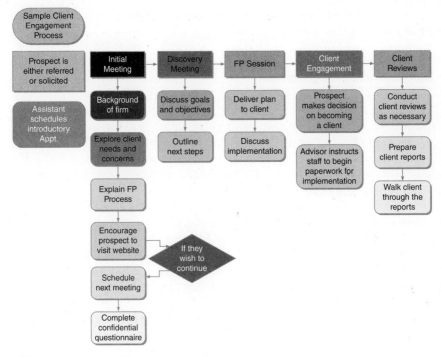

FIGURE 7.2 Sample Client Engagement Process

As can be seen from the flowchart in Figure 7.1, there are five major steps and several other steps under each of the five. Some of these are choices, others are simply sequential steps. However, an employee who might be new to this process could visualize the entire process and quickly grasp the role he or she might have in the process by viewing this type of flowchart, instead of just reading the steps on a page.

Figure 7.2 is another example of a sample client engagement process. This one is a simpler design (shown here in monochrome) but makes use of color-coding. This color-coding could relate to who is responsible for those tasks with a particular color. Again the purpose is to make the job of learning fast and efficient for the people who are doing the tasks.

The color-coding could also be used to identify the importance of tasks. Notice under the "Initial Meeting" major step that the colors change shade slightly with each step. This may simply be used to identify the importance or sequence of steps, not necessarily the person doing them. For this to be effective, you will need to have a consistent approach with each flowchart and develop a color key so that everyone is on the same page with respect to what the color scheme actually means.

BUSINESS CONTINUITY PLANS

One set of procedures that should be a priority for any professional business is the *business continuity plan* (BCP). Also referred to as a *disaster plan*, the BCP is defined by Wikipedia as "that which identifies an organization's exposure to internal and external threats and synthesizes hard and soft assets to provide effective prevention and recovery for the organization, while maintaining competitive advantage and value system integrity." It is also called *business continuity and resiliency planning* (BCRP). A business continuity plan is a roadmap for continuing operations under adverse conditions such as a storm or a crime.

Business continuity plans have taken on greater importance in recent months with a plethora of natural (or unnatural) disasters afflicting many parts of the nation. August and September, typically the most active months for hurricanes, saw several storms rage across various parts of the Eastern and Southern United States, causing widespread damage, power loss, and subsequent business interruptions. Earthquakes, tornadoes, wildfires, flooding, mudslides, and other natural phenomena have created havoc for financial advisors and their clients elsewhere. And, although disaster planning is a large part of the BCP, it is far from the only reason to have such a document in place.

Any potential risk to the continued operation of a firm should be covered in a properly prepared BCP. A few questions to ask yourself might include How prepared is your business to reopen within 24 to 48 hours following a natural or manmade disaster or epidemic? What is your *disaster recovery-time objective* (RTO: your targeted time limit to get critical operations/systems back up and running) following a local disaster? Have you formulated a plan and strategies to limit the impact of risks to your business? Where will your clients, vendors/suppliers go during downtime if your building is destroyed/damaged or employees are quarantined and your business is unavailable for at least some length of time? Does your building have emergency lighting or a generator? What features do you have in place to protect paper files in the event of a fire, water damage, or theft? What would happen in the event that you could not work for a period of time?

The answers to these questions and more could enlighten firms as to their potential exposure and to the overwhelming need to develop a BCP. Advisors often discuss the financial planning process with clients in terms of worst-case-scenario planning. If the worst of all possible circumstances were to arise, could the client reach his or her financial goals? And if the worst is not realized, the client would then be that much further ahead. Yet this same advice is often ignored by the advisor and/or the firm as applied to itself. The objectives of a BCP should be to protect the firm, its employees, and clients, to stay in business no matter what, and to protect the interests of the economy and your community.

The BCP should embrace a planning process that includes:

- Vulnerability assessment
- Risk identification and quantification
- Risk transfer
- Protection and mitigation
- Business impact analysis for interruption of operations
- Plan to mitigate operational and financial risk–based impacts
- Emergency response for these impacts
- Plans to resume, recover, and restore the technological and physical infrastructure to support the firm

Disasters are only one possible cause of a business interruption. The disability or death of key employees of a firm could prove to be just as devastating to a firm that has not preplanned such possibilities (succession planning). Inadequate insurance protection in the event of a disruption due to unforeseen events could prove to be a huge vulnerability. Many firms carry business insurance, but is it enough, and does it cover the appropriate risks? Simply checking a policy for business interruption coverage or extra expense protection could potentially save a firm tens of thousands of dollars.

Perhaps most significantly, the government has established regulations and rules that require firms to establish and maintain a BCP. In April 2004, The Securities and Exchange Commission (SEC) approved rules proposed by FINRA and the New York Stock Exchange (File Nos. SR-FINRA-2002-108 and SR NYSE-2002-35), which require FINRA and NYSE firms to develop business continuity plans that establish procedures relating to an emergency or significant business disruption. In May of that same year, the NASD (now FINRA) filed a notice to its firms announcing Rule 3510, which requires each firm to create and maintain a business continuity plan and enumerates certain requirements that each plan must address. The Rule further requires firms to update their business continuity plans upon any material change and, at a minimum, to conduct an annual review of their plans.

Each firm also must disclose to its clients how its business continuity plan addresses the possibility of a future significant business disruption and how the firm plans to respond to events of varying scope. Rule 3520 requires firms to designate two emergency contact persons and to provide this information to FINRA via electronic means. (In September 2008, the SEC took the unusual step of contacting firms potentially affected by Hurricane Ike to obtain emergency contact phone numbers.)

In May 2006, FINRA reinforced this requirement by issuing a communication to its firms on the violation of Rule 3510. In effect, the ruling states that all firms must maintain a BCP that is in compliance with the 10 elements listed in the rule.

The 10 critical elements of a BCP specified in NASD Rule 3510 are:

1. Data backup and recovery (hardcopy and electronic)
2. All mission-critical systems
3. Financial and operational assessments
4. Alternative communications between clients and the firm
5. Alternative communications between the firm and its employees
6. Alternative physical location of employees
7. Critical business constituents, banks, and counterparty impact
8. Regulatory reporting
9. Communications with regulators
10. How the firm will assure clients' prompt access to their funds and securities in the event that the firm determines that it is unable to continue its business

As comprehensive as this seems, there is one other reason to build and maintain a BCP beyond just following the regulations. Ultimately, mitigating the financial risks associated with a firm being unable to operate for a period of time could be considered as the most compelling for the firm owner(s). Some of those financial considerations might include:

- Establishing and using a temporary alternative location (equipment costs, rent, startup expenses, etc.)
- Routing phone calls to new lines, establishing Internet/e-mail connections, and so on
- Restore costs (rebuilding computers, reinstalling software, recovering electronic files, rebuilding destroyed paper files, replacing equipment, furniture, and other office items)
- Temporary employee costs
- Loss or disaffection of clients due to a perceived violation of trust

■ Violation of compliance issues and/or compromised security and privacy of client information

Many stories have surfaced in recent years dealing with violations of privacy. As an example, in April 2008 a mortgage company that went bust near Denver, Colorado, had its offices cleaned out by the property manager, who tossed laptops, personal files, and other information of some 300 clients into a dumpster. Those files contained Social Security numbers, bank account numbers, and other sensitive personal information. Though it appears the information was subsequently recovered, it points to the vulnerability of such data in the event of a disaster or other event impacting a financial services firm. The scary part is that this happens quite frequently all across the country (Google: "client files found in dumpster"). The threat of identity theft in such situations is very real and very frightening. Therefore, it is incumbent on all financial advisors to prepare a properly written BCP and share it with their clients in an effort to address such issues and alleviate such fears. It is also just a business best practice. For more information on the current regulations and to obtain a free small-firms template, visit www .finra.org/Industry/Issues/BusinessContinuity/.

SOCIAL MEDIA POLICIES

The overwhelming truth is that social media are here to stay. The simple fact is that hundreds of millions of people use social media, and financial advisors are catching on to the benefits of listing their firms on such services. Financial advisors are wise to embrace this new communication medium. But there are a number of issues to be addressed as they embark on a communications strategy. Chief among the issues to be addressed is that of creating a social media policy.

It is certainly a great idea to make use of free advertising media, but in doing so there are a few issues to confront, such as how employees, clients, and others may perceive this use and what rules should be in place to ensure compliance. Such a policy needs to address more than just using social media, and to study how such a use can affect the firm's clients and employees.

Let's first look at what the various steps in creating a social media policy should be. First steps are to reflect on the impact social media can have on your financial practice:

■ Listening is critical.
■ Match the social network(s) to your firm culture.
■ Keep the plan simple.
■ Archive, monitor, and measure.

Having said this, to create a social media policy, several factors need to be considered. There are essentially six parts to a social media policy:

1. **Managing social media accounts:** You will need to determine who is authorized to use, monitor, and communicate through social media sites. You will also need to decide on which social media sites you will be using. You will need to determine what technology may be used to support such use. And you will need to develop a policy on how to deal with negative posts/communications within those sites. If your firm is associated with a broker/dealer, chances are that use of a service such as Facebook may be required to be truncated. By this, you may be required to set up your Facebook account to not allow posts to your wall (for instance).

2. **Company-wide proper use policy:** Developing a social media policy requires a consistent approach to how you use the various social media sites, with the look, feel, and messaging that is used as well as a set of guidelines for you and your staff to follow.

3. **Written and/or visual content:** The actual content of a social media site is critical and should be considered in any social media policy. Such content should reflect similar, consistent messaging shown on the financial advisor's website and other communications. Use of visuals, such as photos, charts, and so on, should be carefully reviewed before posting.

4. **Legal constraints:** Your social media policy should list any and all applicable laws, regulations, and compliance standards (where applicable).

5. **Employee conduct:** This includes employees' personal use of social media. This is a critical issue in that employees could inadvertently mention their affiliation to your firm without your knowledge and create inappropriate advertising through posts made to their sites, without their knowledge or control, or yours. Also among the issues to confront in a social media policy is the use your employees make of social media sites. Whether they like it or not, working for a financial advisor requires them to be subject to certain scrutiny and regulations. Quite frankly, if an employee, for instance, has a personal Facebook site that references his or her relationship with a financial advisory firm, and there are unsolicited posts to that site, it could be construed as advertising (or inappropriate advertising) under current regulations. Employee conduct on social media sites may need to be monitored in some way.

6. **Security protocols:** This is perhaps the most controversial issue of a social media policy. There are now a number of tools available to assist firms in policing and/or monitoring social media use.

Some of the tools you may wish to consider are:

- **Hootsuite** (www.hootsuite.com)
- **Seesmic** (www.seesmic.com)—observing social streams from connections and followers (social media dashboards)
- **Sprout Social** (www.sproutsocial.com)—provides an analysis of social presence and followers
- **Bit.ly,** (www.bitly.com)—tracks the links you share with other websites, offers a link redirection service, and offers two ways to evaluate your social network and identify influencers
- **Peer Index** (www.PeerIndex.com)
- **Klout.com** (www.Klout.com)
- **TweetDeck** (www.tweetdeck.com)—monitors Twitter accounts and was actually developed by Twitter
- **Social Motus** (www.socialmotus.com)—a platform for social media marketing and monitoring
- **Vocus** (www.vocus.com)—yet another monitoring tool

For those firms wanting absolute control, keylogger software may be the answer. Keyloggers typically record and/or monitor every keystroke entered by employees. While this is certainly intimidating and may even be an invasion of privacy on one level or another, for firms with security and regulatory concerns, this might be a solution to consider, particularly if the firm discloses its use with employees and others. One such solution (a typical example) that goes way beyond the keylogger type functionality is a program called Interguard (www.interguardsoftware.com).

Interguard offers a suite of services that include:

- Listing all websites visited
- E-mail and any/all webmail
- Instant messaging/chat
- Social network sites visited and activity on those sites
- Keystrokes typed
- Web searches
- Application use
- Alert words (such as flagging words like *guarantee*, etc.)
- Screenshots

Among others, Interguard also provides an additional layer of services such as:

- Web surfing
- Program usage

- Storage, movement, and handling (deleting, retrieval, and modifying) of critical files (data)

While Interguard is used as an example, there are many such programs available, and the number is growing. Before investing in such software, you may wish to check with your institution, custodian, broker/dealer, or other support firm to see if they already have a solution in place or if they offer such solutions to their advisors/reps at a discount. Many broker/dealers already have such tools or are in process of developing them for their field reps. Understanding what the institution is monitoring may help better understand what you may need that goes beyond what is already in place.

In developing a social media policy, there are a number of resources available, including templates and services; Advisor Websites (http://advisorwebsites.com/blog/social-media/creating-a-social-media-policy-for-your-organization/) offers resources to financial advisors looking to develop a policy. Wired Advisor (www.wiredadvisor.com/resources/advisor-compliance/#) is another firm that offers such services. There are many others.

Quite simply, developing a social media policy is only the first step. Using social media requires effort, diligence, and an ongoing commitment to keep up with the communications. It is not a static solution. Similar to running a blog, someone has to keep up with it. It is a constant, consuming task, and, if you are serious about using social media in your firm, you need to make a substantial commitment of time and, to some extent, expense to optimize its use.

USING TECHNOLOGY TO STANDARDIZE CLIENT SERVICE PROCEDURES

Most advisors use some form of categorizing clients in an effort to identify service levels, and so on. However, many of those same advisors often exceed or, worse, ignore those guidelines for providing service to clients. If those financial practitioners took the time to analyze the costs and revenue consequences of nonstandardized client service, they might realize that they are hurting themselves and their practice from a net profitability standpoint. Fortunately, there are tools to help them deliver those service standards that are both efficient and maintain consistency with the potential for higher profits.

One key to delivering consistently high-quality service geared to match the types of clients and their needs might be to develop and use a relatively simple categorization of clients. On a recent visit to a financial advisory practice, I was introduced to a financial advisor's system of client categories that had 19 different levels of service. Given such variables as assets-under-management breakpoints, whether the client was also a financial planning client, whether the client was using insurance products, or any of a number of other variables, 19 different service levels is simply too much, not only for the advisor's staff to keep track of, but for clients to have a clear understanding of what they are entitled to. While it is important to keep track of these variables, it is not necessary to account for all of them in developing distinctly different levels of client service.

Simple is often better, especially in determining service levels. A financial advisor's staff will find it much easier to understand and apply a simpler system, and clients will appreciate the clarity. Many firms use a color-coding system consisting of perhaps five colors (e.g., platinum, gold, silver, bronze, etc.) with each representing a service category. Most client relationship management softwares have the ability to add such categories to the client record. In practices where it is important to differentiate assets-under-management (AUM) clients from financial planning clients (FP), adding an *A* or *FP* to the end of the color category name would most likely suffice.

But, what about those firms who have combinations of fee-based services? For this, the firm may wish to create a hybrid fee structure and then create a fee numbering system that could be added to a CRM database as a keyword or *user-defined field* (UDF, or *custom field*). An example of this is shown in Table 7.1.

Many firms that might use this type of hybrid fee schedule would probably not need all 15 categories. Table 7.1 assumes that both financial planning and asset management services are provided.

Once the service fee structure is determined, it is necessary to decide on a service-level structure. For this, financial advisory firms have several different variables that can come into play. Consider the example shown in Table 7.2.

With the service schedule shown in Table 7.2, the amount and type of services provided are tied to the profitability of the client. The concept is to gear services to provide the highest level of service and communication to the clients who deliver the highest revenue amounts to the firm. Granted not all Platinum clients (for instance) may want to meet four or more times a year, but it is important that they know they could. And keying the type and amount of work that is associated with the service level makes the task of determining client profitability that much easier.

Client touches could include a number of items, such as birthday cards, anniversary cards, Thanksgiving cards, milestone cards, "How-are-you-doing?"

TABLE 7.1 AUM and Financial Plan Fee Schedule

	Assets Under Management				Financial Planning		Highest Total Fee 1st	Highest Total Renewal
Category	Beginning	End	1st year	Renewal	1st year	Renewal		
1	1,000,000	1,499,999	1.00%	$13,499.99	$ 3,000.00	$1,500.00	$17,999.99	$14,999.99
2	1,500,000	1,999,999	0.90%	$16,199.99	$ 3,500.00	$1,750.00	$21,499.99	$17,949.99
3	2,000,000	2,499,999	0.80%	$17,999.99	$ 4,000.00	$2,000.00	$23,999.99	$19,999.99
4	3,000,000	3,499,999	0.70%	$22,049.99	$ 4,500.00	$2,250.00	$28,999.99	$24,299.99
5	3,500,000	3,999,999	0.60%	$21,599.99	$ 5,000.00	$2,500.00	$28,999.99	$24,099.99
6	4,150,000	4,649,999	0.60%	$25,109.99	$ 5,500.00	$2,750.00	$33,399.99	$27,859.99
7	4,800,000	5,299,999	0.60%	$28,619.99	$ 6,000.00	$3,000.00	$37,799.99	$31,619.99
8	5,450,000	5,949,999	0.60%	$32,129.99	$ 6,500.00	$3,250.00	$42,199.99	$35,379.99
9	6,100,000	6,599,999	0.60%	$35,639.99	$ 7,000.00	$3,500.00	$46,599.99	$39,139.99
10	6,750,000	7,249,999	0.60%	$39,149.99	$ 7,500.00	$3,750.00	$50,999.99	$42,899.99
11	7,400,000	7,899,999	0.60%	$42,659.99	$ 8,000.00	$4,000.00	$55,399.99	$46,659.99
12	8,050,000	8,549,999	0.60%	$46,169.99	$ 8,500.00	$4,250.00	$59,799.99	$50,419.99
13	8,700,000	9,199,999	0.60%	$49,679.99	$ 9,000.00	$4,500.00	$64,199.99	$54,179.99
14	9,350,000	9,849,999	0.60%	$53,189.99	$ 9,500.00	$4,750.00	$68,599.99	$57,939.99
15	10,000,000	10,499,999	0.60%	$56,699.99	$ 10,000.00	$5,000.00	$72,999.99	$61,699.99

TABLE 7.2   Service Schedule Example

Service Level	Meeting Schedule	Report Frequency	Online Tools	Communications
Platinum	Unlimited times/yr	Quarterly	Advanced access to client lockbox	20 touches
Gold	Up to four times/yr	Quarterly	Advanced access to client lockbox	15 touches
Silver	Up to three times/yr	Semiannual	Basic access to client lockbox	10 touches
Bronze	Up to two times/yr	Annual	Basic access to client lockbox	5 touches
Copper	Once per year	Annual	No access	2 touches

phone calls, client appreciation events, and much more. With these types of touches, financial advisors may be able to create workflows in their CRM software to coordinate with the service levels. Then, by using search functions in the software, they can identify those clients who would be eligible for the associated workflow and bulk-assign it when necessary. Redtail Technology (www.redtailtechnology.com), Junxure (www.junxure.com), Protracker (www.protracker.com), Advisors Assistant (www.climark.com), Interactive Advisory Software (www.iassoftware.com), and most other CRM softwares are more than capable of handling this with existing tools. If you are using a version of Salesforce (www.salesforce.com), you may be required to add on a workflow component, depending on the version of Salesforce you are using.

With respect to Redtail and Junxure (for example), it is possible to create preformatted search lists (using Boolean search characteristics) so that each time you click on the list it creates an up-to-date list of clients, even if new clients have been added since the last time the list was used. This is a big efficiency boost and saves time for an advisor's staff in preparing a list.

There are also standalone softwares available for workflow management, if your CRM software does not happen to have such a tool already included. One such solution is called Integrify (www.integrify.com/). Integrify is a cloud-based solution that offers easy access and use and comes with a 30-day free trial. Another interesting choice is from the makers of QuickBooks. Intuit Quickbase (http://quickbase.intuit.com) offers easy setup, customizable reports, and an included mobile access solution and also offers a 30-day free trial. For the more technology-minded user, ProcessMaker (www.processmaker.com/) offers an open-source solution for workflow and business process management. There are tons of others, but these three might be a good start for searching.

Having a workflow management option inside of an advisor's CRM software, though, is still preferred, as it makes the task of tying those workflows to client records so much easier and more efficient. The next chapter deals more specifically with workflow management.

SUMMARY

Chapter 7 explores the importance of having well-defined procedures in a financial practice. Steps are outlined on how to develop those procedures using proven techniques such as mind mapping and the construction of flowcharts. Studies have shown that employees may be able to learn procedures quicker if they have the ability to visually see the steps, as opposed to simply writing them down in a list.

Additionally, the chapter explores business continuity plans (BCPs), which can serve to ensure that operations continue even when disaster strikes. With frequent examples in recent years, environmental and other factors that could potentially cause an interruption of business due to flooding, power outages, and building damage (as in the case of tornadoes or hurricanes) must be taken into account in such plans. Developing office-shutdown procedures, alternative location assignments, and so on are what a properly developed BCP should address.

Finding ways to standardize client service is recommended as it ensures consistency in the delivery of those services and it demonstrates reliability to the client. Developing client service tiers is a necessary part of this effort. Most advisors have identified different categories of clients, such as Platinum, Gold, Bronze, and so on, as a way to understand what the differences in client service delivery will be in each of those areas. However, what is rarely done is calculating the amount of resources expended on, time devoted to, and costing of the service delivery tier. In some cases, advisors will discover that they may be unprofitable in one or more client service tiers because they have not taken the time to identify the true cost of the service tier delivery compared with the net profitability.

One of the newest ways to address this issue is a new software called Fee4Service. This solution looks at the service tiers from a variety of perspectives, including the employee involvement from a time and cost standpoint, the use of other resources (such as meeting room use, paper and ink costs, technology use), and other factors, and then develops a costing page for each service tier that relates to an automated profit-and-loss statement (P&L) generated inside the software. It also looks at these service tier net profits measured against the financial and strategic goals of the firm. Fee4Service software is offered exclusively in the United States by EfficientPractice.com.

CHAPTER 8

Workflow Management Systems

If there is one aspect of a financial advisor's daily operations that has drawn questions in light of relatively new computer software offerings, it is workflow. Workflow management is a key way to ensure the smooth and efficient operation of a financial practice while permitting staff to accomplish common sets of tasks associated with a workflow. Workflow management systems vary, but one aspect they share in common is the establishment of a series of tasks that generally can be configured to be automatically assigned based on the completion of a prior task or workflow task set.

The advantage of these systems is the avoidance of missing steps in a workflow process and allowing things to slip through the cracks. Consistency and timeliness in accomplishing sets of tasks, particularly where it involves communications with the client, are important aspects of increasing the profitability and decreasing the costs associated with the practice. The reduction and/or elimination of errors and duplication of tasks are other potential advantages.

So, if it is clear that workflow is such a great benefit to financial advisory practices, why is it not more universally used? One reason may be the complexity involved in developing workflow procedures. Another may be the misperception that establishing standardized procedures in a firm detracts from the customized nature of the relationship with the client.

To better understand and apply the concept of workflow to your financial firm, it may be necessary to first understand what workflow is, how it works, and what steps are needed to build workflow systems in your office.

One simple definition of *workflow* is that a workflow consists of a sequence of connected steps. It is a depiction of a sequence of operations, declared as work of a person, a group of persons, an organization or staff, or one or more simple or complex mechanisms. *Workflow* is a term used to describe the tasks, procedural steps, organizations or people involved, required input and output information, and tools needed for each step in a business process. A workflow approach to analyzing and managing a business process can be combined with an object-oriented programming approach, which tends to focus on documents and data. In general, workflow management focuses on processes and activities rather than documents. A number of software companies make workflow automation products that allow a company to create a workflow model and components such as online forms and then to use this product as a way to manage and enforce the consistent handling of work. For example, an insurance company could use a workflow automation application to ensure that a claim was handled consistently from initial call to final settlement. The workflow application would ensure that each person handling the claim used the correct online form and successfully completed their step before allowing the process to proceed to the next person and procedural step. In financial services, this could be translated into a workflow process for investment trading, outlining the steps necessary to perform and document the trading process with automated process steps and assignment of tasks to the appropriate employees charged with the responsibility of completing those tasks.

A *workflow management system (WFMS)* is the component in a workflow automation program that knows all the procedures, steps in a procedure, and rules for each step. The workflow management system determines whether the process is ready to move to the next step. Some vendors sell workflow automation products for particular industries such as financial services, insurance, and banking or for commonly used processes such as handling computer service calls. Proponents of the workflow approach believe that task analysis and workflow modeling in and of themselves are likely to improve business operations. Having an automated task assignment within the workflow environment means substantial gains in efficiency and less likelihood of steps being missed or critical functions being delayed because someone neglected to follow up or assign the next task.

The development of a workflow should have at least three steps: (1) a *strategic planning* step, which might include developing a mind map that can sort through all the random thoughts associated with workflows and organize them in some way, (2) the *organizational step*, in which a flowchart or other similar tool might be used to depict the flow of activities/tasks/events associated with a particular workflow task set, and (3) *written steps* in the workflow.

A *mind map* is a diagram used to represent words, ideas, tasks, or other items related to a central key word or idea. Mind maps are used to generate, visualize, structure, and classify ideas, and as an aid to studying and organizing information, solving problems, making decisions, and writing. The constituent elements of a mind map are arranged according to the importance of the concepts. Elements are classified into groupings, branches, or areas, with the goal of representing semantic or other connections between portions of information.

By presenting ideas in a radial, graphical, nonlinear manner, mind maps encourage a brainstorming approach to planning and organizing tasks. Though the branches of a mind map represent hierarchical tree structures, their radial arrangement disrupts the prioritizing of concepts typically associated with hierarchies presented with more linear visual cues. This orientation toward brainstorming encourages users to enumerate and connect concepts without a tendency to begin within a particular conceptual framework.

Some financial practitioners already use mind maps as a tool with their clients to help organize the clients' priorities with respect to their financial and life goals. However, mind maps should also be considered as an outstanding tool for the financial practitioner in looking at the workflow processes within his or her practice.

For purposes of illustration, a mind map might look like the one shown in Figure 8.1.

If you do not already have mind-mapping software, you may wish to check out www.mindjet.com, www.mindgenius.com, or the free version, http://freemind.sourceforge.net. Using the free version, you can learn how such a program can benefit you and your firm before outlaying any substantial software cost. Once you reach a certain level of proficiency, you may find it makes sense to purchase a more full-featured product. Many financial advisors have found success with the aforementioned Mind Genius software.

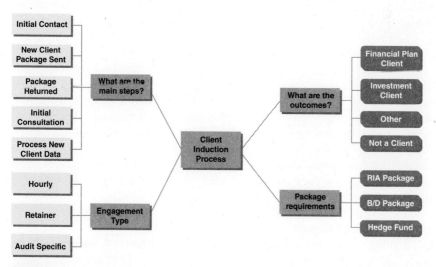

FIGURE 8.1 Mind Map

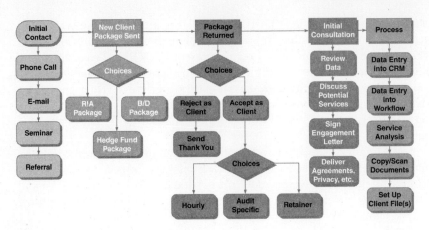

FIGURE 8.2   Sample Client Induction Process

If you already own a version of SmartDraw (www.smartdraw.com), you may already have mind-mapping capabilities. The beauty of mind mapping is the ease with which you can rearrange blocks of ideas/information/topics to create an organized approach. Once organized, you may wish to transfer this to a flowchart to better understand and depict steps in a structural format for a workflow process.

Flowcharting is done to illustrate steps in a series of tasks associated with a workflow. There are several flowchart programs that can be used for this purpose, including the aforementioned SmartDraw.

Figure 8.2 is an example of such a flowchart. This one shows a variety of elements within each task set.

Developing flowcharts that visually depict workflow task sets in a financial practice is a great training tool for new employees. Many people learn faster by visual references, rather than just lines of text describing the workflow steps. Having both published in a procedures manual (electronic or printed) gives the firm an outstanding training and reference tool. This is not just advantageous for the new employee. It can serve as a reminder to those who perform such workflow tasks on an irregular basis or who are needed to step into a role vacated by a recently departed employee or someone on vacation.

There are at least four possible types of task sets: *sequential, non-sequential, decision trees,* and *loop-backs* (see Figure 8.3).

Sequential tasks are tasks that are accomplished one right after the other. In workflow management programs, generally the system "fires" (begins) the next task based on the successful completion of the previous

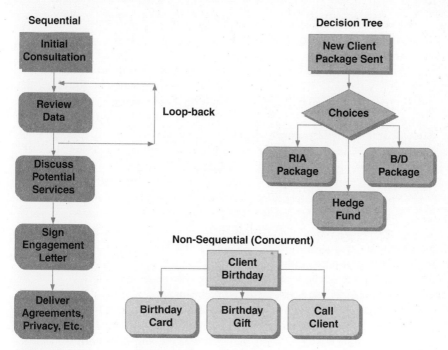

FIGURE 8.3 Four Types of Task Sets

task, and so on. In non-sequential (concurrent) tasks, you may have several tasks that need to be accomplished all at the same time. This would be where the completion of one task could trigger the automatic assignment of several tasks at once. In decision trees, what happened in the prior task might determine which of a list of future tasks must then be accomplished, and the system could automatically create the appropriate next step(s) based on the how the prior step was completed or determined. Loop-backs are where a process is interrupted for some reason and must be restarted from an earlier point. An example of this might be the insurance underwriting process, where during the process it is determined that the contract must be a rated policy. In this example, it may be necessary to loop-back to the application step to apply to a different carrier in hopes that they might not rate the policy, causing a higher premium.

These four typical choices are easy enough to understand. The reality of complex workflows, though, is that a workflow task set could be comprised of several different types of tasks, adding to the confusion in developing the workflow.

There is also the issue of tying workflows to a database. With some client relationship management software programs (CRMs), workflow features are available and can be directly tied to the associated client database. This offers several advantages in that if one needs to check on the status of a workflow for a particular client, it can usually be found in the client's record. Advisors Assistant (www.advisorsassistant.com), Junxure (www.junxure.com), ProTracker Advantage (www.protracker.com), Redtail (www.redtailtechnology.com), Upswing (www.upswingcrm.com), Goldmine (www.goldmine.com), and several others contain workflow features (albeit on differing levels of sophistication). However, workflow is not exclusive to CRMs. There are standalone workflow programs, and workflow features can be found with such document management software as Laserfiche (www.laserfiche.com). One potential drawback to using workflow that is solely associated with a particular function (such as document management) is that it ignores the potential advantages of a broad-based solution that could be applied to every aspect of the firm's operations. However, in cases where the workflow is solely surrounding document management (for instance), such a solution makes sense.

Another standalone workflow management system comes from a company called Perfectforms (www.perfectforms.com). Perfectforms is a standalone workflow management solution that can handle simple-to-complex workflow processes. The issue for some financial practitioners with respect to nonintegrated solutions (not integrated with their CRM software) might be the unwieldy aspect of running a workflow process that must be manually reentered as activities into a CRM database. For this reason, it is recommended, where possible, to use integrated workflow systems (integrated within a client relationship management program if possible).

Another key aspect of efficiency in the use of workflows is in the management of the workflow process. Most workflow software products have reporting capabilities that can simplify the process of managing people and resources. Having the ability to view a list of outstanding workflows and/or completed workflows can free a manager from having to constantly ask employees what work is going on in the office. Having the ability to generate FYI type e-mails can also help; however, in busy offices this can quickly become a burdensome list of e-mails for a manager to have to sift over each day. In those cases, generating a dashboard-type reporting system or building lists for daily viewing is preferred.

In reviewing the lists, it is quick and easy to spot areas where slowdowns are occurring, which can focus a manager's attention on those items for follow-up and review. It may help in spotting training opportunities or system bottlenecks as well. For the system to work well, managers as well as staff must be trained in how to use it effectively.

According to James Carney, CEO of By All Accounts, software "should work like a refrigerator." By this he means that software should be easy to use, work the way it is expected, and not require the user to understand how it works as much as that it works. With a refrigerator, we only want to be able to organize it to find things easily and see that it keeps our food and beverages cold. We do not necessarily need to know how the compressor works. In workflow software, the goal is to make the process of accomplishing sets of tasks easier and more efficient, as well as simplifying the management process.

In the end, how efficient workflow can be in a financial advisor's practice is going to depend on the buy-in by all parties involved in the process. With that goal in mind, firms should consider conducting a strategic planning session with employees that focuses on workflows. In such a session, the agenda might look like the following:

Workflow Planning Session

1. **Introduction:** Fleshing out the concept of workflow management, how it works, and how it can benefit the firm and its employees.
2. **Identify the potential workflow task sets:** Group discussion on the workflow task sets that could be created inside a workflow management system (this might involve the use of mind-mapping software).
3. **Develop the tasks:** List out the various tasks that are inclusive to a task set. In doing this, identifying who does what and when is important. Also, the group needs to define the time required of each step, the method of completion, and the identification of the next step(s) in the workflow process.
4. **Results and benefits:** To gain the most buy-in from employees, it is important to describe the benefits not only to clients and the firm, but also to the employees doing the work.
5. **Management oversight:** It is also extremely important to outline management's responsibilities in the workflow process. Employees need to understand how management will oversee the workflow process, how they can spot issues and be able to lend assistance, and so on.
6. **Follow-up:** It is also important in this session to set a predetermined schedule (say quarterly) to revisit the workflows to ensure that what was set up originally continues to be the most efficient way of doing things.

Three questions to be answered in developing workflows should be:

1. Is it simple?
2. Does it work?
3. Are your employees consistently using them?

If the answer to any of those questions is no, then the workflow management system should be reengineered. According to the American Mathematical Society, Gödel's theorem applies: "No matter how perfect or complete a system, rule, or principle, it will generate anomalies at its margin that do not fit in its boundaries. Efforts to enlarge or change the system to allow for anomalies will only make it inconsistent. Thus, all systems are inherently incomplete." Recognizing this, a firm can do its best to create workflow processes with the knowledge that it is always going to be a work in progress.

PROJECT MANAGEMENT WORKFLOWS

Considering the custom nature of services provided by financial advisors, one question that could emerge is whether a project management workflow process is a viable concept in firms that provide financial services to their clients. The answer is an unqualified yes. But, before we expand on that answer, a quick review of what project management is and how it can be used should be explored.

Project management is a term applied to the process of performing a series of steps and managing resources to bring about accomplishment of a particular project or goal. To be effective, the process should be outlined with goals, objectives, steps, assignments, accountabilities, and timelines. Along the way, a look at potential obstacles and ways to overcome those obstacles should also be woven into the process.

It is a clear objective of project management to ensure the project is completed on time and on budget. Therefore, timelines and financial considerations should be part of the process as well. The problem with all of these variables is that, without a process template or checklist to follow, the project could easily be derailed, delayed, or simply fail. So, one step that can ensure success is to have an effective platform to accomplish the project within stated guidelines.

Let's look at a potential use of project management within a financial practice. For this example, let us choose the development of an informational seminar as the project. The goal of the project might be defined as generating new business. One objective might be to define how much new business, measured by new client acquisition. With those parameters in place, it becomes necessary to develop the steps in the process. In this case, the following steps might apply:

1. Develop the seminar presentation.
2. Develop a seminar invitation letter.
3. Purchase or acquire a list of prospects to send the letter to.

4. Set up a seminar meeting location (perhaps a restaurant or conference location).
5. Arrange for refreshments, hors d'ouvres, and so forth.
6. Send out the seminar invitation letter.
7. Make follow-up phone calls to respondents.
8. Hold the seminar.
9. Follow up with attendees and solicit initial consultations.
10. Review the success of the project (evaluate new client acquisition).

These 10 steps must then be fleshed out in terms of what tasks are associated with each step, who is responsible for what, and what are the accountabilities. There must also be a timeline established to control and monitor the timeliness of the project. There may also be a need to train employees in the tasks associated with the project, tying their efforts to the overall goal of the project.

Perhaps most important, and often lacking from financial advisors' projects, is a cost-benefit study to determine the cost of such a project weighted against the benefit in dollars. As an example, if, on the one hand, after all the dust settled, the cost of the seminar program came to $2,500 (for instance), but the benefit resulted in one client purchasing a product (such as a commission-generating product) that earned the firm $1,500 on a onetime basis, it could be concluded that the results did not match the expectations, calling into question the viability of the project or its parts. If, on the other hand, the project resulted in several profitable clients generating continuing fees and/or other revenue, it could be concluded that the project was a great success. Either way, wouldn't the financial advisor need to know this going forward? Even if the project resulted in less-than-stellar profits, it might compel that advisor to address components of the project, such as the seminar topic or quality of the invitation list.

There are many projects that might be beneficial to financial service firms, such as:

- **Document management system:** Developing an electronic document storage and retrieval system to complement or replace your existing paper-based files. This is a project that could conceivably take several months or longer to implement; one of the chief concerns is to success-fully implement such a system while keeping costs down and minimiz-ing staff interference with their daily activities.
- **Office relocation:** Accounting for all the steps and costs associated with an office move, including timelines, employee responsibilities, and so on.
- **New employee hiring process:** Includes steps such as advertising, interviews, background checks and psychometrics, specific skills, or other testing.

Very important to such projects is keeping track of all of the steps in the process. You may wish to consider a project management software program. The obvious choice in this instance might be Microsoft Project. It is generally regarded as the standard among project management software programs. However, for limited projects requiring simpler, more focused project management steps with less complexity, MS Project may be too much (or too expensive with the standard version priced at $549.99, professional $949.00).

Developing a spreadsheet with a checklist of items is another choice. With a Microsoft Excel spreadsheet, one can develop the steps with details and links to progress charts, and so forth. The process becomes more visual and can be replicated with other projects in the future. What might be lacking with this choice is the interactivity with other, divergent softwares such as your client relationship management software.

Redtail Technology (www.redtailtechnology.com), a web-based platform for CRM, offers an integrated checklist that could be used for simpler project management. This effective tool does integrate with the larger client database and can be monitored by management, integrated with the calendar, and so on. While not a workflow management feature (Redtail also offers workflow management), this is a simple, yet efficient tool for use in keeping track of projects and the steps involved in successful accomplishment of a project with an eye toward staff accountabilities.

Another viable choice is a software program called Project KickStart (www.projectkickstart.com). Project KickStart Pro, Version 5, is a terrific product that offers all the features needed by financial advisors (and other businesses) without the complexity or cost associated with Microsoft Project (Version 5 is priced at $299.00). The software offers a quick, intuitive interface that can learned in about 30 minutes or less. You can be up and running with the software right away. Interestingly, there is an export feature that permits you to export to MS Project, if needed. Of greater interest, though, is the export feature that creates a Power-Point slideshow instantly from your completed project setup. For training purposes, this is a very powerful feature that requires no effort or extra expertise on your part to create a set of slides that fully illustrate your project and all of its parameters. KickStart offers several other export capabilities to popular software programs such as Excel, MindManager, ACT, and others.

Beyond just setting up goals, objectives tasks, and assignments, the software also creates a fully adjustable Gantt chart for timeline monitoring. It can be viewed under a number of different ways (weeks, months, quarters, etc.), depending on the length and needs of the project. And, you can save the projects to be used as a template for different projects in the future, cutting down on keystrokes and development time. In short, Project KickStart saves you time and money while providing an efficient platform to set up and monitor your firm's projects.

WORKFLOW SYSTEMS: EFFICIENT METHODS FOR TRACKING TASKS IN THE OFFICE

One nagging question that keeps arising is whether the services provided by financial advisors are profitable given the amount of time, effort, and resources expended to provide them. Despite how often this question comes up, the answer is frequently unknown. This may be because practitioners simply haven't taken the time to add up all the costs associated with various tasks performed on behalf of the client.

As an example, a recent discussion with a financial advisor revealed that his firm was charging an average of $750 for a standard financial plan. Yet, a subsequent audit of the workflow processes required to produce the plan determined that it took the firm (consisting of the financial advisor and a para-planner) about 20 hours to complete the plan. Given the $150/hour rate normally charged by the advisor (according to him), the hourly cost to produce the financial plan was around $3,000, not $750. Given staff time, printing costs, and paper and binding expense, the actual cost to the firm could be even higher. The argument for continuing to charge the $750 was that they would make up the difference in the asset management fees. This may be true, but the larger questions are: What is the overall impact to the firm for such sloppy workflow tracking? And what is the message that is being sent to the client?

Many firms have begun to consider breaking apart their fee structures in an effort to get a better handle on profitability and to eliminate so-called *loss-leader* services. The reason to create an à-la-carte menu of services is to create a stable cash flow for the practice and to better justify what is being charged to the client. Let's say you have a fee-based financial advisory practice where you charge 1 percent asset management fees and you offer financial planning as a part of overall services that do not incur a separate fee. The advantage of this system is that it is easier to do the accounting and simpler for the client to understand. The disadvantage is that, in a down-market year when assets under management (AUM) might decrease, your fees would go down as well. And it may be telling your clients that the advice isn't worth much. Additionally, many advisors question the wisdom of this practice as it suggests their services are worth less in a down-market year.

The alternative is à-la-carte pricing or breaking out the advice fees and potentially decreasing the AUM fees. The calculated amount of revenue from a client might be the same, but in a down-market year, the advice fees (if flat rate or fixed) could help stabilize an otherwise declining revenue base. And the message being sent to clients is that the advice is worth as much or more when the going gets rough. You may also find your practice being more competitive in the AUM fees (if they are lowered) as compared to other practices in your community.

However, before creating an à-la-carte pricing model, it is a good idea to better understand what is involved in producing the various services offered to your clients. To accomplish this, many firms are turning to workflow systems to set up tasks, track progress, and build accountabilities for task completion.

One such system is already incorporated into a client relationship management software package called Junxure (www.junxure.com). Junxure has action tasks that permit the user to assign a task with time and date stamping. The task can be general in nature or tied to a client record. The task (or action item) can then show up on the assigned employee's action list with prompts. Once completed, the assigned employee can so indicate with a date completed. The record is retained in history for anyone who uses the system to see. With custom reports, an administrator could develop a task accountability report to help in specific task completion studies and to oversee and compare similar tasks performed by different people. Another CRM software package, Act 4 Advisors (www.software4advisors.com/act4advisors.htm), can perform similar functions.

If you use Microsoft Outlook 2003 (www.microsoft.com/outlook), you may wish to check out the task assignment features already included within the program. In addition to creating your own tasks in Outlook, you can create tasks that you assign to others. You do this by sending a task request to someone. (A *task request* is a request sent in an e-mail message asking the recipient to complete a task. If the recipient accepts the task, it is added to the recipient's task list, and the recipient becomes the new owner of the task.) The person who receives the task request becomes the temporary owner of the task. He can decline the task, accept the task, or assign the task to someone else. The good news about this feature is that when the owner completes the task, Outlook automatically sends a status report to the person who originally assigned the task, any other prior owners, and anyone else who requested a report.

On a standalone basis, financial advisors who want to get a handle on workflow processes in their practice without necessarily tying those tasks to client records may wish to look at a simple task management software called Task Anyone (www.taskanyone.com/checklist.html). Each task can be set with a creation date, due date, estimated time, elapsed time during task, and priority, and the task can be assigned. There is room for a note on current status of the task. You can append tasks to master tasks and view or change the hierarchy of tasks. At $9.95 per month and offering discounts for volume purchases, this product is an inexpensive way to get a handle on workflow issues.

If you are interested not only in what your employees are doing when they are working on firm-related tasks, but also in what they are doing when they are not working on company business, there is an office spyware program called Spector Pro (www.spectorsoft.com). Spector Pro provides the ability to record every program (or application) and program window run on the computer you are monitoring. For each program, Spector Pro will capture the name of the person who used the program, when the program was started, and how long the program was running. In addition, Spector Pro will provide even more information, such as how much time the program was actually used. Was the program simply opened and left on-screen, an indication someone might be trying to deceive you into thinking they were working all day in Word and Excel (when they were really surfing the Web)? At $99.95, this could be another tool to monitor your employees and potentially insulate your firm against lawsuits resulting from inappropriate use of company computers (e.g., Internet porn, etc.).

All of these tools mentioned are useful only to the extent that your firm can benefit from the information they provide. Establishing workflow systems, setting accountabilities, and determining the cost of services provided to clients can help with employee management and product (service) pricing issues. The intended result should be to achieve more efficient office operations.

SUMMARY

Developing and using workflows effectively can provide greater operational efficiencies for a financial practice. Once developed, workflows can simplify the process of managing employees, if a workflow management system with management tools is used. However, time must be devoted to the development process to ensure accuracy and completeness. And, employees need to understand and appreciate the value of such a system.

This chapter outlines the development process, from the strategic planning to using mind maps and flowcharts to ensure that the workflows are properly designed. Even more important is having a workflow management system that can automatically assign the various task steps in a workflow process, ensuring that nothing falls through the cracks and processes are completed on time and on budget.

Chapter 8 looks at the fundamentals in developing workflows, such as the different types of completion steps (e.g., sequential, non-sequential, decision trees, and loopback task flows). It is important to be able to account for these different task outcomes, and so selecting software that is flexible enough to do this would be recommended. Fortunately, there are several choices, from integrated solutions inside of a CRM software to standalone workflow management softwares.

PART Four

Design Efficiency

Office Space Utilization

Using your existing office space efficiently can be one of the most challenging aspects of your operations. Often, the cost per square foot of office space demands that you lease as little space as possible. Yet how many financial practitioners use expensive office space to house old files, for instance? As an example, placing older files (dormant client files, aged files, and files no longer in use) in a filing cabinet inside an office space that costs upwards of $20 per square foot per year, when compared with an offsite storage solution for the same space at a fraction of that cost, is an inefficient use of your resources. Yet many financial practices are doing this. Why is this so? Usually, the answer lies in an understanding of the evolution of the practice. Often, a practice starts out as a one-person shop and grows from there. It is possible that, as the practice grows, more file cabinets are purchased to house paper files, and little thought is given to the per-square-foot cost (footprint cost) of placing those file cabinets in an office location.

Consider the following example. A typical 48-inch-wide lateral file cabinet occupies approximately 12 square feet of space. But, considering the drawer-open space needed and walking room around the cabinet, that number balloons out to 24 square feet. If your office has 10 such cabinets, you are using up to 240 square feet of office space. If the space costs $20 per square foot per year, then the cost of placing those files in that space could be $4,800 per year. Compared with an offsite storage location (at least for older files), you could probably get similar storage space for around $1,400 per year ($100 – 120 per month). That means you are wasting as much as $3,400 per year.

The argument defending the use of such space is *access*. Practitioners may say that they find it inconvenient to go offsite every time they want to view a client file. The answer to this is virtual file cabinets (electronic storage solutions) that take up almost no space and offer instant (and often more organized) access to client files and information.

CREATING A PAPERLESS OFFICE

Converting an office to a paperless environment can be a daunting if not overwhelming set of tasks. For some financial advisors, the prospect of such a conversion could entail months of preparation and work. Yet, there are solid reasons to strongly consider creating a paperless office that go beyond environmental reasons. Cost savings, rapid and ready access to files, file sharing with clients and other professionals, and protective backups are only a few of the reasons. There are also ways to mitigate what might seem like lengthy and exhaustive work to complete a conversion. Here are a few steps to help you get there quicker and perhaps with less expense.

Step One: Create a Project Plan

It is important to consider an office conversion to paperless as one part of a larger picture of what you are trying to accomplish with overall office operations. Simply jamming paper into a scanner and sticking the files into a hard drive is nowhere near enough. Consider the development of the file structure, for instance. If your physical files are constructed with tab sections, you may wish to emulate this in your electronic files, particularly those associated with clients. Having a common filing structure means less time for staff to understand it and find files.

In creating the project plan, consider developing a timeline for completion of the project with specific goals at various points in the timeline. Consider also determining the extent of the paperless conversion. For example, some firms may wish to determine a line-in-the-sand approach, where they identify only those files that are current, and not subject to sun-setting rules, to be scanned, and continue to hold the remaining paper files until they can be safely destroyed under IRS and/or SEC rules. For some, this may represent a seven-year rule or potentially more. The reason to consider this is if your office has, for instance, 350 clients with 30+ years of paperwork, attempting to scan all of this could turn out to be a mammoth job that would be not only expensive, but a major time-consumer. For active financial advisory firms, this could mean hiring extra staff just to complete the scan-and-store processes. So the line-in-the-sand approach is intended to take a practical view of what the firm actually needs and can sustain without a major interruption of staff time and without incurring a major expense.

Step Two: Select the Technology

There are literally dozens of choices when it comes to creating a paperless office. The simple truth may be that you already own what you need. In many cases, financial advisors may own equipment and software capable of the task, but may not fully understand or utilize what they have. Software companies have partnered with equipment manufacturers to create combinations of technology and software that can get the job done. However, if those solutions are not compatible with the firm's client relationship management (CRM) software, then it may turn out to be a lot bigger job and more expensive than it needs to be. So the advice here is to do your homework. Investigate your current technology and software to determine if the functionality already exists to create a paperless office environment. Make certain that whatever systems you have are fully compatible. If not, then look at what is out there that is compatible with what you already own.

As an example, if you are using Redtail Technology (www .redtailtechnology.com) as your CRM, Redtail offers a seamless solution called Redtail Imaging that can coordinate with the client files and documents, allowing you to automatically scan and store directly to the document tab in Redtail. Junxure (www.junxure.com) CRM offers a similar functionality as do most other CRMs designed for the financial services profession.

If there is a fair amount of accounting-related paperwork involved, you may wish to look at Neat Receipts (www.neat.com). Neat offers not only a scanning system, but an intuitive software that can recognize the paperwork it is scanning and potentially file it according to its content. NeatDesk is a high-speed, duplex desktop scanner and digital filing system. You can scan receipts, business cards, and documents in one batch while the software first identifies, then extracts and organizes key information. Neat brings scanned documents to life, using intelligent text recognition technology to read and understand key information, and then automatically organizes what it sees. The resulting digital files are useful and usable—easy to find, easy to access, and easy to share. The scanner is capable of scanning at a rate of up to 24 pages per minute and can handle double-sided pages. You can feed up to 50 pages at a time.

Neat also offers a portable scanner for use outside the office or at a client's home or place of business. With their NeatCloud solution, access to files is potentially available anywhere, any time. However, the included software may need to be adapted for use with a CRM. Also, 24 pages per minute, while seemingly fast, can be slow when faced with mountains of paperwork to be scanned.

If speed of scanning is the issue (and why would it not be?), consider the Fujitsu fi-6130z (www.fujitsu.com/us/services/computing/peripherals/scanners/workgroup/fi-6130z.html). It has blinding speed, with up to 40 pages per minute in color, monochrome, and so on. The 6130z has exceptional clarity with 300-dpi scanning resolutions and comes with

Kofax® VRS® Professional and ScandAll Pro 2.0 software. However, this scanner can work with a variety of different document management solutions.

Among those are such industry leaders as Laserfiche and Docupace. Laserfiche (www.laserfiche.com) offers document management solutions for both RIAs and broker/dealer–affiliated advisors. Because Laserfiche provides both departmental flexibility and enterprise control, thousands of leading RIA firms use Laserfiche enterprise content management to create a user-friendly, standardized system for managing client information, company records, correspondence, and even e-mail and social media in a way that's convenient, comprehensive, and compliant.

Using simple but powerful automation tools, Laserfiche accelerates and streamlines business processes, saving time and money while reducing security risks. The Laserfiche Avante software, for instance, includes workflow management features to speed the process of document management.

However, Docupace (www.docupace.com) has made great strides in this marketplace by offering their document management solutions at an attractive price, often discounted through broker/dealer and/or custodians. Docupace claims to be the industry's first web-based SEC/FINRA–compliant paperless processing system.

Docupace is an industry leader in delivering SEC/FINRA–compliant paperless processing systems to financial services firms. Their document management and workflow solution simplifies the process of capturing, organizing, routing, and accessing information. And it is compatible with most current CRM software solutions used by financial advisors.

Step Three: Get Staff Buy-in on the Project

This is critical. Your staff needs to fully understand the scope of the project, the potential benefits to the firm, and, perhaps most important to them, the potential end-user benefits to them. Once the system is in place, they could end up saving hours of labor through automation of document management processes and electronic file handling. If your staff realizes the benefits, they are much more likely to embrace the front-end commitment to make it happen. The firm is much more likely to end up with a more efficient and productive office as a result.

File cabinets represent only a small fraction of space utilized in an office location. Other issues involve considerations for workflow. Placing the desk of the person responsible for effecting investment trades (for example) on one side of the office while having the desks of others who would submit such trades on the other side of the office could mean forcing employees to walk back and forth all day just to pass paperwork. Grouping desk locations of staff who are connected from a workflow perspective can increase work-flow and communications efficiency.

COMMUNICATIONS IN THE OFFICE

Communications efficiency is another aspect of office space utilization. Some have argued that, with intercom systems and e-mail, communications can be maintained regardless of the desk location. This may be true to an extent. However, studies have shown that when talking with a co-worker on the phone or via e-mail, the employee may tend to multitask, which diverts attention from the conversation. There is also the loss of the benefit of nonverbal forms of communication, such as visual expressions, body movements, and so on, which can aid in understanding. An interesting new trend with a limited number of practitioners is the installation of webcams and use of office-wide instant messaging services. When monitored and controlled for business purposes, this can restore some of the benefits of face-to-face communications.

AUDITORY AND VISUAL DISTRACTIONS

Being distracted from your work can be frustrating. It can also cost you and your firm money. Distractions can lead to delays in getting work done, and potentially making mistakes in your work, and can have the effect of disrupting an otherwise harmonious office environment.

Studies have shown that, when distracted from an analytical task, it can take upwards of 10 to 20 minutes to get back on task mentally. Multiply this times the number of given distractions in a given day, times the number of affected employees, times the number of work days in a given year, and you have major roadblocks to efficiency.

Essentially, there are two main types of distractions, visual and auditory. A visual distraction by definition is where some movement in the range of your vision causes you to interrupt your train of thought or current activity. The most common form of this in an office is movement in the office that is observed, often with peripheral vision, which causes the observer to stop what he or she is doing. In an office situation, this could be due to the configuration of the furniture, the height of cubicle walls, or the presence of clear lines of sight from one office to another.

Visual distractions do not necessarily have to originate outside of a person's work area. There are plenty of visual distractions within a person's desk area. Most notable is the computer, tablet, cell phone, or other electronic device. With respect to the computer, simply reading and answering e-mails the minute they show up on your desktop can be very disruptive. Text messages from friends and family members can also interrupt your thinking or analytical work.

An auditory distraction is a noise, loud conversation, or other auditory event that breaks your concentration. Even something as seemingly innocent as a loud copying machine, placed near a desk with someone who is doing analytical work, can provide an annoying auditory distraction.

Multitasking is often lauded as a good skill. Yet studies have shown that there are hidden costs to multitasking that may not be readily apparent. Joshua Rubinstein, Ph.D., of the Federal Aviation Administration, and David Meyer, Ph.D., and Jeffrey Evans, Ph.D., both at the University of Michigan, describe their research in the August issue of the *Journal of Experimental Psychology: Human Perception and Performance,* published by the American Psychological Association:

> *The measurements revealed that for all types of tasks, subjects lost time when they had to switch from one task to another, and time costs increased with the complexity of the tasks, so it took significantly longer to switch between more complex tasks. Time costs also were greater when subjects switched to tasks that were relatively unfamiliar.*

Here are nine common and inexpensive tips to help you overcome distractions:

1. **Tame the phone:** If the phone is a problem, use your assistants to deflect all but the really important calls. Provide resources so that your assistants can handle most of the common matters on their own without requiring your input.
2. **Corral your e-mail:** Stop jumping to answer every single e-mail as soon as it arrives. Dedicate some time blocks each day for managing your e-mail. For example, one session during the morning hours and another one in the afternoon should work reasonably well. Consider setting an auto-responder message telling when you are reading your emails. Most people expect you to react to e-mails instantly, but communicating with them about the way you process your e-mail helps them to understand why you are not getting back to them as soon as possible. You do not need to know the second a new e-mail arrives to your inbox—turn off the notifications (sound, popup windows, etc.). If you have subscribed to various mailing lists, evaluate them critically as to whether you really need to subscribe to them. If not, unsubscribe!

Define rules for certain types of e-mails, so that they are being handled automatically. If you use Outlook, you can define rules for moving e-mails when received into subfolders. By categorizing those folders in order of priority, you will know the folder you should always check first, and so on.

3. **Close the door:** If walk-in distractions are becoming too frequent, shut the door. Scheduling "office hours" or regular meetings with your staff is a simple strategy that can reduce distractions. Your staff and/or co-workers should understand that when the door is closed, you are not to be interrupted (except for emergencies).

4. **Reduce or eliminate clutter:** A cluttered desk and office can be a distraction. Get rid of unnecessary papers and other items you do not need, especially those that are near your main work surface. Not having all of that junk to look at will help you concentrate more on your work.

5. **Play music or work in silence:** Some people concentrate better with soft music playing in the background because it drowns out other noises and distractions. Others prefer more up-tempo music because it helps keep them alert. And some people work much better with total peace and quiet. Studies have shown that certain masking sounds, such as music, can affect the behavior of people. As an example, some department stores use soft, slow-tempo music during the day to cause shoppers to pause or slow their pace of shopping, which increases the likelihood of higher sales. At the end of the day, the music increases speed and tempo, causing shoppers to hurry, which makes the task of closing the store that much easier. Similar concepts can be applied in any workplace.

6. **Get plenty of sleep:** Lack of sleep makes you tired during the day, and being tired can result in an inability to concentrate on your work. The average adult needs 7 to 8 hours of sleep per night. If you're not getting that much, it could be adversely affecting your productivity.

7. **Use a to-do list to help you keep track of what you need to do:** Using a to-do list to capture what you need to do instead of relying on your memory can help you focus and concentrate on the task at hand because you avoid all those distracting thoughts floating around in your head. You don't have to keep reminding yourself to do this or that because you've already captured it.

There are a number of time management software tools you can use to help with this; many are free. Trog Bar (www.priacta.com), Schedu-Flow Online (www.duoserve.com), and Efficient Calendar Free (www.efficientsoftware.net) are three solutions you may want to check out. All three are available from www.download.cnet.com.

8. **Take a planned break:** When your brain is on overload, take a break if possible, but time it to coincide with a natural break in your work or schedule. If you're in a work environment where your breaks are scheduled, try switching to a less demanding task for a few minutes. Anything that gets your mind off of the task you're having trouble with for a short time will help. Then you can get back to it in a more refreshed state.

9. **Reduce or eliminate multitasking:** Unless the group of tasks are associated, simple, and ease to manage, multitasking can actually be harmful to your work and cost your firm money.

Staying focused is vital if you want to be a productive professional. Many distractions can be avoided, and you can improve your focus with some simple adjustments. Once your mind is able to concentrate on the work at hand, you can get it done much more quickly and efficiently, with fewer errors.

OUTSOURCING

Another way to increase the efficiency of an office is through outsourcing certain aspects of business operations. (you may wish to read Chapter 2 for detailed information on outsourcing.)

IMPROVING FIRST IMPRESSIONS

Yet another aspect of office space efficiency is the construction issues surrounding the reception area. Some offices have adopted what might be called the *dentist office design.* This is where the waiting area is separated by a wall with a window (often with a glass partition) separating the receptionist from the people in the waiting area. Studies have shown that this design lends itself to fear and apprehension on the part of prospective clients. Just what are they hiding in the receptionist's area, and why do they need to put walls between the staff and clients? One of the first observations might be that the wall itself takes up a certain amount of floor space that could have been put to better use. Another observation is that by taking down the wall and opening up the space, you just might increase the positive aspects of an open space environment. This could mean clients entering the waiting area would feel welcome and not have the apprehension that accompanies receptionist walls.

Atmosphere in the waiting area is critical to a prospective client's first impression of your firm. Presenting an office environment and culture that is both warm and inviting is an excellent first step to building a positive impression for your prospects and clients. To do this, consider a few tips:

- Use lighter colors for walls, flooring, carpets, and so on.
- Consider placing a small fountain or other water feature in one corner of the waiting area. Bubbling water often is soothing to the ear and relaxes people.
- Ditch the signs that promote services. Don't place a laundry list of products and services in the waiting area. Mutual fund prospectuses or other sales material should be well out of eyeshot. This also means the receptionist area. If a prospect spots large racks of sales material in the waiting/reception area, the message you are sending is you are going to try to sell her something.
- Take out the water cooler, if you have one, in the waiting area. Train your staff to offer a beverage and make sure it is served in a china cup (if coffee) or glass (if a cold beverage). Dixie cups, Styrofoam cups, and so on, send a message that you are running a cheap operation. Prospects want to be pampered and made to feel special. They don't want to feel as though they are sitting in the waiting area of the local oil-change shop.
- Another clever trick to enhance the atmosphere in the waiting area is to place a warming tray in or near the area and put fresh cookies on it just before prospects or clients are scheduled to arrive. When they open the door, they are greeted with the smell of warming cookies. There is nothing quite so disarming as that smell. Avoid microwave popcorn as a substitute. Some people are irritated by that smell (and if you overcook it, the stench is hard to get rid of).
- Keep the "ego wall" out of the waiting area. Having certifications, degrees, awards, and other recognitions is great and can be useful when placed in a conference room or practitioner's office. But, for first impressions, remember the saying: "People don't care how much you know until they know how much you care." Arrange the first impression to be one that conveys the message that you really care about your clients. That first impression is all about them, not you.

Making the most efficient use of your space is not all about squeezing more into less. It may mean creating a brighter, more open, and harmonious office environment that is attractive and inviting, not only to clients and prospects, but also to your staff and yourself.

FENG SHUI TIPS FOR YOUR BUSINESS AND OFFICE

Consider these tips from ancient Chinese philosophy:

- Always sit with a solid wall behind your back to ensure that you have support in your life; never sit with a window behind you.
- In the office always place the fax machine, telephone, and computers in the "wealth area" and "future wealth area" for more business.
- The arrangement of tables and chairs should be in a harmonious position so that *chi* (energy) is able to flow smoothly.

- If you wish to be the leader in your industry, place a dragon on the right-hand side of your desk facing toward the window or the door. The dragon can also look into your water fountain. A dragon always chases after a pearl, thus the window; the fountain can signify the pearl.

- If you own a shop, try to place the till in your wealth corner, even your petty cash tin. Order books can also be placed here with Chinese coins held together with red ribbon.
- You should not have any cactus or sharp-looking plants in your office as these plants have small sharp leaves and therefore cause *shar chi* in the office. The chi that rides on the wind will have to pass through them, causing chi to be fierce and sharp.
- If your staff always fall sick in that area, then use a metal wind-chime made of six or seven metal rods about one foot long; the sound of metal is the best Feng Shui cure. (A metal sculpture or metal object would not be as effective although they are also metal in nature.) Place a hanging crystal sphere to activate chi or disperse negative chi.
- In your office, never have the main door opening into your table as the chi coming in will hit at your face causing you not to have good luck but instead more obstacles and problems. Reorganize your office.
- In a manager's office, you should try not to choose a room with two doors, because the chi will come in one door and go out the other.
- The chi from the main entrance of your office should not meet a wall inside the office. This is because once it hits the wall, the chi has to turn, which causes it to slow down; hence your businesses will be slow and not vibrant. Try using a hanging crystal in your office entrance; this will enhance chi.
- Do not place the photocopy machine near the main door. Heat near the main door is frequently not preferred and causes the chi to be hot and dispersed easily, as more people are likely to walk in and out, thus carrying chi in and out too fast because the chi is not allowed to stay long enough.
- Do not place a paper-cutter machine next to the main door. A cutter machine cuts papers. Therefore, if located here, it will cause staff to back-stab each other and fight if one is not careful.
- Do not place an empty vase next to the main door; once it enters your office, the new chi will be sucked into the vase, leaving nothing much for the environment.
- For corporate clients, a fish tank placed in the wealth area is the best for great results and success. However, there are strict criteria for the fish tank that one has to follow.
- The company signboard should be in the wealth area so that no other competitors can be strong enough to beat you at your game.
- Place an indoor fountain in your wealth corner to activate chi. This also has medical benefits.
- Do not have clutter in your office; desks must be kept tidy and clutter-free. This is so important, an office in China would not have paper trays on desks, and most American companies now employ the same approach.

- Place a hanging crystal in your window. This will activate chi, as well as looking fantastic. When the light hits the crystals, they produce the most amazing rainbows.
- Three-legged Toad god: This figure is used for attracting wealth and abundance. Place this wonderful creature near your front office entrance, facing into your office for luck and wealth, or place it in the wealth sector of your office to magnify your wealth luck. Always leave the coin in its mouth.
- Crystal ball: Apart from looking into future, you can place one on top of the phone to encourage more business calls, also to attract wealth and good luck, a great all-around cure that every office should have.
- Fu dogs, male and female: These protective animals are placed near the doorway of your office to protect from evil influences. They are a symbol of valor and prosperity.

- Ba Gua mirrors: If you have any negative energy directed at your front office door, these Ba Gua mirrors will disperse the negative energy.

Granted, not everyone accepts the mystical concepts behind these tips. However, according to Chinese culture, these have an immediate and long-lasting effect on the office environment. They are, at the very least, conversation starters.

SUMMARY

Chapter 9 explores office space utilization. The simple fact is that most professional offices waste space in one way or another. There may be inexpensive ways to make better use of your space. As an example, using your (potentially) high-priced-per-square-foot office space to store long-term files that are rarely if ever accessed is an incredible waste of space and money.

Therefore, exploring a paperless office solution may be one effective means of regaining that space for more useful purposes. This chapter outlines steps you can take in a project to transform your office into a paperless environment. Care must be taken in how this is done, as it can become an overwhelming project unless certain parameters are put in place. Some offices may choose the line-in-the-sand approach. This approach suggests that you choose a date after which all paperwork is to be transformed into electronic form. This technique is preferred as it is less cumbersome than attempting to transform many years of paperwork.

Despite SEC and FINRA rules on file retention that suggest a maximum of, let's say, seven years to retain certain types of documents, many advisors have those documents still on file after 20 years. The sun-setting approach would transfer those older files to a less expensive but secure storage facility, and the newer stuff would be retained in electronic form.

Additionally, the chapter reviews communications in the office as well as auditory and visual distractions. What might seem like a minor issue, such as an auditory distraction, can be a serious impediment to efficiency in the office. Studies have shown that when interrupted by such a distraction, it can take up to 20 minutes to mentally get back on track, if you are doing an analytical task. Once you calculate how often this occurs and how many employees are affected, the loss of time can be significantly high.

Chapter 9 also looks at ways to utilize the office space to improve first impressions. And, it offers a list of Feng Shui tips. Granted, not everyone accepts the validity of Feng Shui. But, studies have shown that when Feng Shui is employed in an office, the office environment and harmonious working relationships improve.

CHAPTER 10

Efficient Branding

Hardly a day goes by that someone does not offer some new idea on how to market a business. Most such ideas go the way of other fads by fading quietly away. Others seem to stick, and still others grow in popularity over time. Given profit constraints on the financial services profession and competition battling for the same block of clients, it is not surprising that financial advisors seek new ideas and alternatives when it comes to marketing their financial practice. The fact is that there exists a certain level of sameness in this profession that makes the task of differentiation that much more difficult. However, there is a popular movement that promises to change all that. Dubbed the *Blue Ocean Strategy*™, this concept embraces a systematic approach for making the competition irrelevant. A book written by W. Chan Kim and Renee Maubourne, appropriately titled *Blue Ocean Strategy* (Harvard Business School Press, 2005), suggests theoretical approaches to creating "blue oceans" of *uncontested market space* ripe for growth. The book, written in 2005, sold over a million copies in its first year and is now being published in 39 languages, which suggests that this is one of those ideas that is growing in popularity.

BLUE OCEAN STRATEGY

The concept of the Blue Ocean Strategy (BOS) is that the entire marketplace of potential clients (customers) is divided into red and blue oceans. The red oceans are characterized by accepted industry boundaries (basically all of the industries in existence today) whereas the blue oceans represent all the industries not in existence today, the unknown market space, unaffected by competition.

To illustrate red oceans, as the market space gets crowded, prospects for profits and growth are significantly reduced over time. Products become commodities or niches, and cutthroat competition turns the ocean bloody— hence, the term *red ocean*.

In blue oceans, demand is created rather than battled over. There is significant opportunity for profitable and fast growth. In blue oceans, competition is deemed irrelevant because the rules of the game are waiting to be made. Blue Ocean is an analogy to describe the wider, deeper potential of market space that has yet to be explored and/or exploited.

The three conceptual building blocks of BOS are (1) value innovation, (2) fair process, and (3) tipping-point leadership. Clearly, the lynchpin of the Blue Ocean Strategy is *value innovation*. Of the three, this is by far the most difficult to achieve, as it requires a fair amount of research and labor (not to mention creativity) to accomplish. In essence, value innovation is the simultaneous goal of achieving a new approach, service, or offering combined with exceptional value for what is offered. A Blue Ocean is created when a firm innovates a new product or service that provides value to both the client and the firm.

Fair process is offering the service with the recognition that it is done with fairness to those who are served. To be a true Blue Ocean, this new offering must raise and create value for the market while simultaneously reducing or eliminating features or services that are less valued by the current or future market. But, to make this concept work and be sustainable, firms must find ways to deliver the product or service efficiently and with a reasonable profit. This may not be as difficult as developing the product or service itself simply because in a new market space, pricing is largely an unknown element. Fair process is accomplished by following three *E* principles: engagement, explanation, and expectation clarity. *Engagement* means involving individuals in the strategic decisions that affect them by gaining their input and permitting them to be involved in the development of ideas and assumptions. Some financial advisors have approached this by creating an advisory council made up of a select group of existing clients. *Explanation* simply means that everyone involved and/or affected by a new differentiation strategy understands why the strategy has been put into effect. *Expectation clarity* requires that, after a strategy is set, the financial advisory firm clearly communicate the new strategy, requirements, and/or benefits.

Tipping-point leadership merely states that once the service or offering is designed and offered to clients, a continuous effort is made to promote it, even in the face of initial resistance.

The book offers several examples, including Dyson vacuums. Inventing a whole new way of vacuuming, Dyson then set about the task of building a marketing program that solidified its place alone in that market space. The vacuum process, one that had been largely the same from company to company for years, was turned on its ear by a company offering a vacuum with no filters to clean and a Dyson ball that turns on a dime. In the beginning, no competitor was prepared to counter the campaign. Dyson could effectively charge whatever they wanted for their vacuums and did. Most were twice the price of other manufacturers, and yet they captured significant market share because it was a new idea that captured the imagination of the consumer.

Another example is the story of Pitney Bowes, whose CEO at the time, Michael Critelli, created the Advanced Concept & Technology Group (ACTG), which identified and developed a new machine that enables people to design and print their own postage from their desktops: *value innovation that embraces Blue Ocean thinking.*

Examples of Blue Ocean Strategy abound, but one in particular is the case of a financial advisory firm that was searching for such a solution. When confronted with the concept of differentiation, research was done, and it was discovered that the owner had a special-needs child. Even more, he had joined support groups for families with special-needs children and had even begun to gain some of those families as clients. Yet, despite this, he had not explored pursuing this as a marketing niche or as a differentiation strategy. Once the decision was made, the website was retooled to reflect this specialization, and marketing materials and advertising were refocused on this concept. Within 18 months, the firm experienced a remarkable growth from families who had long searched for a financial advisor who specialized in this area and had up to that point been unable to locate one. Although this is an isolated case, it is an excellent example of how differentiation can make a substantial difference in a financial practice.

While these examples are interesting, a bigger question is how this can be applied to a financial advisory firm. The answer is pretty much the same as it would be for any industry or profession. The Blue Ocean Strategy begins by plotting a strategy canvas that is a diagnostic tool designed to illustrate the range of factors on which a profession competes and plots this against the offering level that clients receive across all these key competing factors. A strategy canvas might look like the one shown in Figure 10.1.

To plot a new value curve, there are essentially four key questions that must be answered in order to challenge a profession's strategic logic and business model:

1. Which of the factors that the profession takes for granted should be eliminated?
2. Which factors should be reduced well below the profession's standard?
3. Which factors should be raised well above the profession's standard?
4. Which factors should be created that the profession has never offered?

The answers to the first three questions should lead to the fourth question's answer. However, that fourth question is the hard one. It speaks to

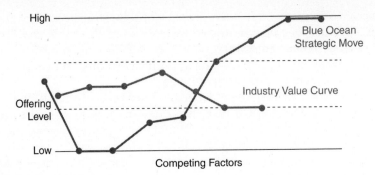

FIGURE 10.1   Strategy Canvas
Source: Courtesy of www.blueoceanstrategy.com.

the concept of differentiation. The underlying principle of the Blue Ocean Strategy is, at its core, differentiation. If a firm is solely concerned with creating and ignores the cost factors, it will have accomplished nothing. Often, those companies that embark on a path of blind innovation without regard to value, cost, or client appeal find themselves losing rather than gaining.

One example of this might be a firm that chooses to produce a comprehensive quarterly report for clients with fancy charts, graphs, tables of figures, comparisons to indexes, and lengthy commentary without first determining if such a report is warranted or even desired by the client. The "build it and they will come" philosophy does not always work in an environment where the firm has not taken the time or care to determine need or want in their clients or prospects.

Differentiation is about acquiring new business and not just strengthening existing client relationships. If, in the course of doing business, it is determined that a firm works well with a certain group of clients, it could explore a brand identification that targets that particular group. This focus on specialization is a form of differentiation. Another example is to identify specific characteristics (experience, education, special certifications, etc.) of the firm principals and build a brand structure based on this as the case for differentiation. The key is to find that certain unique aspect of the profession that can be solely owned or used by the firm.

Presenting yourself to the public as "an advisor who serves the needs of families with estate issues" is not a sufficient case for differentiation. There are probably 50,000 firms that do the exact same thing. Presenting yourself as "an advisor who serves the unique needs of families with special-needs children and their estate planning issues" would be an example of a step in direction of the Blue Ocean. Building systems, procedures, and deliverables that meet the needs of such a practice efficiently and profitably while correctly targeting the client group with a compelling brand awareness that captivates those potential clients would fully embrace the Blue Ocean Strategy.

Many firms have reached a point in the evolution of their practice where they realize that in order to compete successfully, they need to find a niche market for their services. The concept is often referred to as *differentiation,* and it requires a certain amount of research and introspection to accomplish. It may also require doing some soul searching on what the goals are for your practice and your life.

One example of differentiation involves a financial advisor in Texas. James Poe, MSFS, is the chairman and founder of Texas Retirement Specialists (www.texasretirementspecialists.com), a registered investment advisory firm (RIA). Texas Retirement Specialists has offices in Ft. Worth and Dallas, Texas. In a phone interview with Jim, he explained his unique niche: "investing for women." Jim mentioned that he is the proud father of six daughters, four of whom work in his practice. Additionally, Jim is the host of two radio shows (one in each city where his offices are located), and last year his firm generated over $20 million in new business.

Jim, who has more than 35 years' experience in the financial services profession, recognized a trend among families nearing or at retirement. According to him, husbands were generally selecting a maximum payout for themselves from Social Security (and other retirement income sources) without consideration of the impact on their spouse. As statistics have shown that women outlive men, it struck Jim that the women would be left with considerably less (or potentially nothing) following the passing of their husband.

For this reason, Jim created a unique set of services that embraced a focus on maximizing retirement income for both husband and wife. This includes a focus on retirement income sources, asset accumulation, tax planning, and estate planning, in what he referred to as his RATE system. Jim indicated that he has uncovered 81 different ways to maximize Social Security. And, he mentioned that, in meeting with clients, highlighting the issue of Social Security makes the women in those client groups pay attention. In his words, "They get it."

Jim's passion for this was undoubtedly influenced by his large and extended family of women. He has written a number of books on the subject and has authored a number of articles in the *Erickson Living Tribune*. In addition, James Poe has been quoted on Fox Business News. But he credits his radio shows for delivering the largest percentage of new clients to his practice.

The story related by Jim Poe should resonate with financial advisors who are struggling to define their differentiation strategy. Often, the answer is in front of them in that some experience or influence in their life and/or work can be the key to a unique niche for their practice. To uncover it may take a certain amount of introspection and self-evaluation.

The question is: What steps need to be taken to develop and implement this type of differentiation strategy for your firm? The first step is to do a certain amount of soul-searching and introspection. Exploring your passions and your strengths/weaknesses can go a long way toward uncovering where your niche may lie.

A relatively simple Blue Ocean exercise to uncover your value innovation is called *ERRC*, which stands for *E*liminate, *R*aise, *R*educe, and *C*reate. The steps are in this order:

1. Eliminate: Write down those aspects of your profession that could be eliminated that are those factors that the financial services profession has long competed on. This might include parts of your service offerings, fee structure, marketing methods, and so on.
2. Raise: Write down those factors of your practice that could be raised well above industry standards, such as communication methods, frequency, and so on.
3. Reduce: Write down those things that could be reduced well below industry standards (obviously without violating compliance rules, B/D requirements, etc.).
4. Create: Make a list of things that could be offered to your clients and prospects that the financial services profession has never offered. This might involve specialization in untraditional areas such as the aforementioned "families with special-needs children," or working with high-net-worth single executive women nearing retirement (the point is to seek out your niche, based on working with groups of potential clients in other, unique professions/lifestyles in which you may possess a unique knowledge).

What lies at the center of these four lists should be your unique value innovation, that aspect of your profession on which you may be able to retool your firm to specialize or capitalize.

Once identified, the next step is to implement a strategy that not only delivers the new innovation, but provides a fair process in delivery. Fair process simply means delivery of products and services in a way that ensures fair value and recognition by the recipient of the quality of those products and/or services.

To provide this, one way to start is to develop a value proposition or statement of the value and fair process. An example of such a statement might be as follows:

> *XYZ Company provides financial security through a unique use of expertise in nontraditional investments diversified in a multi-asset-class portfolio to provide stability in the value and growth of a client's investments consistent with their current financial needs and future goals.*

The purpose of such a statement is to be able to articulate the unique value innovation that can be delivered to the client and to do so clearly and succinctly.

The final step is to retool your website, marketing, and promotional materials to align with this message and to then deliver that message using tipping-point leadership.

Based on the book, *The Tipping Point: How Little Things Can Make a Big Difference* (Little Brown, 2000), the *tipping point* is an examination of how change happens all at once as the result of a constant reinforcing element, such as a consistent and continuous message. The message is delivered to clients and prospects through a variety of venues and is consistently pushed out there over time. In other words, this is not a "try it for a while to see what happens" approach. We are talking about a long-term consistent approach to deliver that unique value innovation, one that is far more likely to yield substantial results than any other method.

Examples of this can be found everywhere, but one in particular involves a financial planner who placed a two-inch advertisement in a local newspaper's once-a-week business section. The ad showed her photo and the simple phrase "thorough and resourceful financial planning" along with the phone number. This ad was run for probably 20 years. It fueled the substantial growth of this very successful firm over those years. In preparation for retirement, the ad was pulled and then changed later with the firm's new principal, her son. Yet, when people continued to see her on the street they would remark that they just saw the ad in the paper. It had been so consistent that it was embedded in the memory of any and all who read that publication.

While newspapers may not be the most popular advertising medium with financial advisors, the same approach can be taken with websites, social media, e-mail campaigns, radio and television spots, and a variety of other venues.

Using the value innovation approach can help you to identify your niche and also provide a highly efficient and easy-to-maintain system to dramatically increase the influx of new clients to your practice.

MARKETING SERVICES

There are now outsourcing services available to assist advisors with referral marketing. One such service is FiPath (www.fipath.com). FiPath offers the Refer My Advisor program. The program, designed by advisors for advisors, was developed as an effective system to get referrals from clients without ever asking face to face. The program eliminates the need for end-of-appointment asking for referrals, and for cold calling to random leads, and provides referrals only to prospects who are not only expecting, but wanting your call. It is a proven solution for advisors wanting and needing new prospects without the worry and work associated with obtaining them.

Another choice in this category is Boulevard R's advisor marketing program (AMP) (http://ampformarketing.com/). AMP helps turn more prospects into clients by:

- Creating a sense of urgency and moving more prospects to a second meeting
- Presenting your solution in a timed way so that you close more prospects

One final thought with respect to marketing involves touches. Many advisors have abandoned certain marketing programs after one or two tries if the results are not immediately apparent. This is a mistake. Studies have shown that on average 21 touch points with a prospect produce the most consistent results. In advertising, the consistent approach, such as placing an ad in a weekly business newspaper over a period of a year, will provide a cumulative effect. Over time, the results aggregate to a much higher prospect count than if you merely submitted the ad from time to time. It does not have to be an expensive, large, or even colorful ad—just consistently there, according to the research.

Again, while newspaper advertising may be less popular these days, the Internet, websites, referral systems, and social media loom as viable and efficient replacements.

EFFICIENT WEBSITES

In the financial services profession, many practitioners have created websites. However, for most, this is an afterthought and lends itself to the concept of *sameness*, particularly when the advisor chooses to use a website service that offers templates for financial advisory firms.

Most of these sites have simplified the means of creating a website fast. Often they include features such as stock lookups, investment research, and so

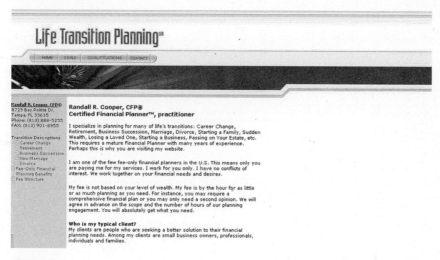

FIGURE 10.2 Life Transition Planning

on. The question that a financial advisor should be asking is, "If my clients are using these type of tools, why do they need me?" Because they are so prevalent throughout the financial profession, these websites tend to all look the same. If the firm is trying to establish a case for differentiation by developing a niche market, using this approach in its website is a step in the wrong direction.

There are effective ways to use these website hosting services that can set the firm aside from others. It just takes some planning and forethought. But before we go there, let's look at some real examples.

Figure 10.2 is an example of what is often called a *brochure website*. There is no visual interest and little reason to go to this website, much less scroll through the pages of the site. In short, it is boring. Another example of a brochure-type website is shown in Figure 10.3.

The example in Figure 10.4 shows even less visual interest. When someone is visiting your site for the first time, studies have shown that you have approximately 7–8 seconds to attract his attention and compel him to go beyond the home page. Otherwise, he hits the back-button and searches for another site.

In Figure 10.4, the firm is using a website provider's template. And, while it smacks of sameness to many other sites, it is clearly better than the previous two examples. Even so, inclusion of research tools, market summaries, and financial calculators would suggest that, again, if clients are using these tools, why do they need an advisor? Another observation

Four Seasons Financial Planning

Financial Planning - Asset Management - Retirement Planning - College Funding - Estate Planning Spending Plans - Risk Management - Tax Planning - Trust Management - Charitable Giving - Business Planning - About Us - Financial News - Contact Us

Four Seasons Financial Planning, Inc. is an independently owned association of Certified Financial Planners with allegiance only to their clients.

The emphasis of the firm is steadfastly rooted in the conviction that a comprehensive financial plan is essential, both to the client and to the firm, if effective financial management is to be accomplished.

Of equal importance to the firm is the conviction that products utilized to realize clients' goals, whether stocks, bonds, insurance, or other financial tools, should be utilized because of their appropriateness to the seasons and goals of our clients' lives. Consequently, the firm utilizes only fee based asset management. Fee based insurance products are utilized where possible and appropriate.

The firm maintains a full spectrum of financial management products with the exception of those requiring allegiance to a producer (proprietary products).

Our Philosophy

There are seasons of our lives: those we expect--children, education, retirement, old age--and those we fear--sudden deaths, lost jobs, separation from loved ones. We all have dreams, both large and small. At Four Seasons Financial Planning, we believe that only through proper planning can we fully enjoy each of life's seasons and the pursuit of each dream. With proper and appropriate saving and preparation for the unexpected, our clients can enjoy spending the funds they have allocated for today without guilt and fear for tomorrow.

Businesses, like our lives, have seasons, with many of the same pitfalls through infancy, adolescence and maturity, and must be planned for accordingly. We serve our business clients much as loving parents do, guiding and preparing them, freeing their owners and employees to do what

FIGURE 10.3   Four Seasons Financial Planning

Financial Factors, Inc.

Fred Forbes, Certified Financial Planner & Certified Senior Advisor

COMPANY
Welcome
Background
Products & Services
Links
Retirement
CONTACT
Email Us
Request Info
Insurance Quote
Locate Us
INFORMATION
Personal Finance
Retirement
Short Takes
Taxes
RESEARCH
Market Summary
Calculators

Welcome to our firms web site.

Please feel free to explore this site to gain better understanding of our firm and how we help our clients plan for and meet their financial goals.

If you have come looking for an investment manager to manage your companys retirement or pension plans, you have come to the right place. If you are a successful individual looking for a financial counselor, you to are in the right place. Financial Factors, Incs purpose is to create and preserve well being for both businesses and individuals.

After talking to us, you will know you have been heard. We begin by determining our your financial and personal goals. We will create a plan that will help you achieve your goals. Money management is not an easy process. Effective money management involves two important components: managing your investments and preserving your wealth. Our goal is to create financial solutions and provide an extraordinary amount of personal service.

We invite you to use the Contact tools on the left-hand menu to ask any questions. Let us know if there is any other information you would like to see on this site.

Thanks for stopping in. We appreciate your visit.

FIGURE 10.4   Financial Factors, Inc.

FIGURE 10.5   Website "Before"

is that the website is all about the advisor and not the client. If you are trying to capture the imagination of a potential client, it is necessary to give those potential clients visuals and content that they can identify with.

To see the transformation of a website to a compelling message of differentiation, look at the before-and-after shots of this website in Figures 10.5 and 10.6.

Here we see that the website has been redesigned clearly to create identification with the client and not the advisor and not the stock market. This is a terrific example of creating differentiation and presenting visuals that might compel a first-time visitor to the site to dig deeper into the site and to hopefully call for an appointment.

FIGURE 10.6   Website "After"

SUMMARY

Chapter 10 looks at ways in which you can position your firm to deliver a branding message that differentiates you from the competition. The concept of the Blue Ocean Strategy is discussed along with ways in which you can utilize the techniques inherent in this strategy to increase your ability to attract and retain new clients.

Along with this discussion is a listing of various marketing systems that can be complementary to your firm's marketing efforts. Typically, marketing may be way down the list in a financial advisor's skill levels. Financial advisors have had the opportunity, through education and experience, to become very skilled at working with clients, managing clients' money and financial goals, and working with clients on estate planning needs. But the profession has done a poor job of preparing those same advisors to be good business owners. Marketing is a key element in the success of any business. If you do not have the skills to do it yourself, outsource it to the experts.

The chapter concludes with a look at some financial advisor websites with an eye toward reshaping your website to be consistent with your marketing message and positioning. The examples show that many financial advisory firms use very simple or template websites that contribute to the overwhelming sense of sameness that pervades the profession. Yet there are simple, inexpensive ways to restructure a website to deliver your message of differentiation. In effect, you can transform your website to deliver a Blue Ocean message of value innovation that so compels your website visitors that they contact you following that visit.

Afterword

Operational efficiency is more than just a theory; it is an achievable goal for a financial practice. But, there is more to reaching that goal than taking a piecemeal approach to it. For many financial practitioners, opportunities for new software, new systems, and new techniques lend to a tendency to use a piecemeal approach. However, in the long run, you could be doing more harm than good for your firm. Software, for instance, if chosen in a vacuum, without consideration for how well it may interact with other software already in use, could prove to be detrimental to operational efficiency by adding more work for staff to deal with the lack of interaction. New systems if introduced without proper planning and training could face a firewall of pushback from employees wedded to the old ways to doing things. And decisions on procedures, workflow, and policies, if not tied to technological systems could be counter-productive to the operations of an office.

Therefore, a holistic approach makes the most sense. The Profit-Driven Architecture, referenced in the introduction, is a visual way to approach a holistic solution for operational efficiency (see Figure A.1). It is not realistic to assume that you can introduce new pieces of the operations to a practice without it affecting the other parts. And it is not rational to assume that by doing things the same way over and over again, you will achieve different results. In fact, that is one definition of insanity. Albert Einstein once defined

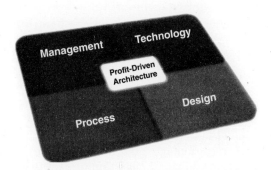

FIGURE A.1   The Profit-Driven Architecture

159

it by saying, "Insanity: doing the same thing over and over again and expecting different results."

Management, the first of the four blocks of the Profit-Driven Architecture, is nearly impossible to make more efficient in a firm that is growing rapidly without utilizing other blocks in the architecture. Technology can play a tremendous time-saving role in managing staff and resources, but only if it is used properly and in balance with the other areas of operations. Technology, for all its innovation and cool new gadgets, is only useful when used in concert with proper management and process controls. Office design must take into account more than just aesthetics. It should examine the most advantageous layout of offices, furniture, and equipment relative to people that use them and the security issues surrounding them.

Chapter Two reviews some techniques to measure success. It is the tendency of financial advisors to look at their gross revenue and then look at the hard costs of doing business. In other words, decisions affecting the practice may be made based solely on expense and/or additional revenue; whereas, there are many other impacts that must be considered.

As an example, there are many theories on how to accurately calculate the return on investment for software used in a financial practice. The business owner often misunderstands the actual amount of investment into a software product or service. As a result, true ROI calculations for most small businesses are skewed.

Most financial advisors make their mistake in this most necessary calculation, because they do not properly value their own time. Indeed, "resources" include cash money *hard dollars*. But, they also include "human resources" or "time" *soft dollars* along with the impact on firm capacity opportunity costs.

Some financial advisors will finally run ROI calculations including the human resources, and suddenly realize that there are many more factors to consider than simply the dollars involved.

A traditional calculation of ROI might be this basic formula:

$$ROI = [(Payback - Investment)/Investment)] * 100$$

However, this calculation fails to detail what is meant by payback, much less the actual investment involved. So, to better understand the full impact, several factors need to be considered.

On the cost side, there is not only the cost of the software solution, but also the cost of transitioning to the software. Many firms charge fees for installation, customization, and migration of data to the new platform. These fees are generally in addition to the actual software subscription costs.

But there are also the soft-dollar impacts to consider, such as the advantages gained from operational efficiency as well as increased capacity and time management. Reductions of errors, which add to increased workloads and, often client frustration, are another example of soft-dollar impacts.

IMPACT ON PRODUCTIVITY, PROFITABILITY, TIME MANAGEMENT, AND FIRM CAPACITY

The impact on productivity of using a holistic approach is unmistakable. Let's look at the example of a firm that has substantial clients. In this example, the firm employs four para-planners to do quarterly reports for their clients. On average, each para-planner is tasked with doing somewhere around 60 to 80 of these reports each month. And each report takes on average about six hours to complete.

The reason for the length of time lies in the way the reports are constructed. Each report is constructed from several data sources that must be hand-stitched together, then assembled into a three-ring binder for presentation to the client. Because the sources of data do not talk to each other, the process is mostly manual and laborious.

By utilizing a holistic approach, involving the true integration of data from all sources, this process was reduced from six to eight hours to under one hour. The resulting time savings translated into increased capacity for the firm. Despite their rapid growth, they were not required to hire additional para-planners. Time management was made considerably easier as well.

IMPACT ON BUSINESS VALUATION

Whenever a firm can point to higher levels of efficiency, profitability, and capacity, this not only provides a venue for higher growth for the firm, but increased firm value. For those firms looking to transition to retirement through some sort of succession plan, providing such efficiencies can mean a much higher valuation that can facilitate the decision to retire.

Well defined and documented business processes can also impact firm value. A firm that has defined, developed and documented their critical day-to-day functions in a systematized workflow process is far more valuable than a firm that has not. This could easily translate into a valuation far higher than that of a firm without defined, documented, and repeatable "best practices." Turn-key operations offer the principals an easier and faster exit if desired rather that an extended work-out period.

FIRST CASE STUDY

For the purposes of illustrating this, we will use a real case, but change the names to protect the identity of the associated firm. For this purpose, we will refer to the firm as the XYZ firm.

The circumstances of XYZ firm are that they currently use Product A (a web-based client relationship management software) for some client data storage needs. They also use Product B (a financial planning solution). Additionally, they are using Product C for portfolio management and reporting. Even more, they are using a separate portfolio rebalancing solution (Product D), and they are also using a separate asset allocation program (Product E). They pay separately for the use of a client portal as well (Product F). The combined total cost of these software solutions is $. This is due to a large number of client records (around 600+). The firm also discovered that additional add-on programs were needed to facilitate data transfers between these various software, add-ons that proved to be less than user friendly or complete in transferring all needed data, which required several manual steps, cut and paste routines, etc.

A comparison of costs/benefits was calculated using a holistic application, Interactive Advisory Software (IAS). (E-money Advisor is a similar type solution.) And, while many firms may benefit from an integrated solution such as IAS or EMoney, this type of solution may not be appropriate or warranted for every advisory practice. In many cases, using divergent softwares that are capable of sharing data can offer greater flexibility for the firm. But for this case study, IAS is used for illustration purposes only.

In this case study, the client benefitted from saving across hard dollar, soft dollar, and opportunity cost. (*The appendix contains a study undertaken by the firm ActiFi that explores these comparisons as well*).

Hard dollar: eliminated the use of divergent software solutions and add-ons

Soft dollar: greatly improved the access to data across all functionalities and eliminated repetitive keystrokes and tasks on the part of employees working inside the platform.

Opportunity cost: Used time saved to increase proactive client out-reach and create more value-added services

The calculation shows that a savings among 7 employees totaled an average of 2.85 hours per week (in a reduction of staff time). Using a $30 per hour standard (approximates an employee earning at the rate of $18 per hour, plus tax contributions and benefit costs to the firm), the savings in staff hours equals (in this example) approximately 1,000 hours per year or

$30,000. This is a soft-dollar impact in that the firm is already paying staff for this, but it is a measure of the inefficient use of staff time that would be eliminated with the new platform. Presumably, that time could be better spent on client-related activities, assuming that the firm has additional capacity to take on more clients and, consequently, more work.

The comparison also has to take into account the costs involved in a conversion to the new platform (a first-year cost only). Setup fees, minus incentives offered by a custodian, will equal $5,600 in this example. Additionally, the costs incurred by the firm in additional workload during the conversion process, such as time involved in data entry and customization equal $10,000. (This is also a soft-dollar impact in that no out-of-pocket money is involved, just redirection of staff duties).

The resulting calculations are shown in Table A.1.

As compelling as the above calculations may be, there is much more to consider in the decision to move to a more efficient platform environment. Setup and conversion costs occur in the first year only. After that, the comparison of costs is more dramatic. The example above shows a cost savings over $53,445.00 in the first year, even with those setup and conversion costs included. However, in the second year, the difference widens to $63,445.00. And that difference continues from that point on year after year. For many firms, that could be the salary of two employees.

However, even this is not the only thing to consider. There is much to accomplish in converting to a new platform. Employees, particularly those who fully understand and may have had a hand in developing the existing systems, may resist changing to a new platform. They may view the aggravation of setting up new systems, databases, and so on as more egregious than staying with the existing systems, despite their potential inefficiency. Firm owners need to consider this impact and the possible push-back by employees. However, in the end, a firm needs to be run as a business, with all factors considered in the decision-making process. Certainly, the long-term impact in this example far outweighs the short-term inconvenience, assuming there is any. And it more than justifies overruling any objections from employees wedded to the old, inefficient ways of doing things.

And remember that the above case study only looks at one part of the four operational areas of the Profit-Driven Architecture, technology, and really only one aspect of it. Factoring in gains in efficiency from better management techniques, automated workflow management, more efficient office environment and branding/marketing solutions that embrace the firm's differentiation messaging all contribute to significantly higher levels of productivity, net profitability, efficiency, and increased firm value.

TABLE A.1 XYZ Firm Cost Comparison

Divergent Software		Holistic Integration Software Solution		
Item	Current Yearly		1st Year	2nd Year
Product A: CRM Software	$ 5,460.00			
Product B: Financial Planning	$ 4,200.00	Software	$ 59,100.00	$59,100.00
Product C: Portfolio Mgmt	$ 45,000.00	Setup	$ 5,000.00	
Product D: Rebalancing	$ 31,500.00	TDA covers	$(15,000.00)	
Product E: Asset Allocation	$ 1,548.00			
Product F: Client Portal/Website	$ 2,337.00			
Third-party add-ons	$ 2,500.00	Conversion**	$ 10,000.00	
Workload add*	$ 30,000.00			
Total	$122,545.00	Total	$ 69,100.00	$59,100.00

*$30,000/year savings on employee cost reductions, based on workflow translates, into increased capacity, reduced stress, better work environment, more efficiency.

This is based on $30/hour times 1,000 staff hours/year (approximately 20 staff hours reduced per week). This example uses a firm with seven employees (staff hours saved = 2.85 hours per employee/per week).

**Conversion cost is a calculation of soft-dollar impact using staff hours to input data, customize, etc.

***$30/hour standard based not only on actual salary, but all benefits, staff support, technology, etc.

SECOND CASE STUDY

Let's look at another case study that encompasses more than just a single issue. In this case study, an exhaustive comprehensive evaluation was performed on the financial practice. The practice is a dually registered financial advisory firm with seven employees. In the course of accomplishing the evaluation, the following recommendations encompassing the four areas of the Profit-Driven Architecture were made:

#	Action Item	Timing
1	Management Efficiency: Consider adopting a concierge style of practice. Consider re-aligning staff responsibilities consistent with the operational areas and teams identified in the staff retreat, with the identified team leaders. Consider adding an ongoing advice component for a fixed fee and integrate this with a hybrid pricing structure. Consider using a Redtail software program to its fullest extent. Consider setting up a schedule template. Consider setting up a tracking system to monitor acquisition of assets and fee revenue from a firm perspective. Consider developing a business plan that embraces branding and differentiation strategies. Consider developing detailed position descriptions and a three-point evaluation system that utilizes objective criteria to apply to the performance and behavior of your employees on the job. Consider developing a managerial oversight system with detailed reports and quick look screens that can provide instant information on all activities performed within the practice.	These items should be phased in over the next four months
2	Technical Systems Efficiency: For client relationship management (CRM), we recommend Redtail. Redtail Technology offers an online ASP type platform.	Workflow management customization of Redtail and website redesign are priorities here and should be done ASAP.

(continued)

#	Action Item	Timing
	For the purpose of providing a better financial and estate planning software solution, consider using MoneyGuidePro.	
	For backup purposes, consider using MozyPro.	
	You may wish to consider using a lockbox type technology on your website. To do so, we recommend that you consider using the lockbox feature on Orion's Platform.	
	For risk profiling, we recommend using FinaMetrica (www.finametrica.com).	
	Consider adding an IPS Solution to your suite of financial planning softwares. For this purpose, we recommend IPS Advisor Pro (www.ipsadvisorpro.com).	
	Consider adding the newest version of Adobe Acrobat Professional to everyone's desktop.	
	Consider redesigning your website and promotional materials with branding and strategic planning results in mind.	
	Consider setting up an account at Mobile Assistant for more efficient note taking.	
3	Process Efficiency:	Employee position descriptions and evaluation system are priorities and should be done soon.
	You may wish to consider redeveloping the employee handbook (policy manual).	
	You may wish to identify and then begin the work on developing procedures for each task accomplished within the office.	
	You may wish to consider adding these procedures to the workflows inside of Redtail to automate the various steps in a process and ensure that there are no drops.	
	Taking into account the operational areas that were identified in the staff retreat, consider developing a team structure as it was outlined.	
	Consider developing a three-step program for managing your employees.	
4	Design Efficiency:	Cooling element is highest priority.
	Consider adding a cooling element to the server closet ASAP.	
	Consider eliminating clutter throughout the office.	
	Consider adding softening elements to the office environment to create a more harmonious workplace.	

The actual evaluation report went into considerable detail on each and every one of these recommendations. But, for the sake of simplicity, these are the basic points of the report. (Please note that these recommendations are specific to this firm and do not apply generally to other firms.) Each efficiency evaluation is customized to fit the specific situation and needs of the firm being evaluated.

Taking this to the next level, to properly understand the impact on the financial practice, forecasting was done as illustrated in Table A.2.

TABLE A.2 Recommendations and the Potential Financial Impact

Item	Hours/ month Recovered	Yearly Potential Impact	
Workflow management system	89	$ 37,380.00	Reduction of time associated with establishing or chasing down work, etc.
Operational construct and teams w/staff leader	26	$ 10,920.00	Office staff time reduction
Reduction of office clutter	14	$ 5,880.00	Reduction of every staff members' time
Mgmt oversight systems —mgmt. reporting	32	$ 36,923.07	Reduction of Fred's time
Better time management	78	$ 32,760.00	Increased capacity from efficiencies
Data sharing—CRM, port mgmt, client reports, etc.	96	$ 40,320.00	Time reduction of six employees who handle data entry (estimate)
	335		
Total potential* financial impact yearly		$164,183.07	
Total annual reported gross receipts 2013		$126,025.00	
Percentage of total		130.28%	

*Financial impact may be felt in increased time and capacity for the firm as well as hard dollar savings.

Net Profit
Potential Impact

Building efficiencies into your business has a cumulative effect on financial impact. Table A.2 is a quick study of the potential impact, financially, to your firm. It should be pointed out, however, that there is a psychological impact and a social impact to increasing efficiency. These may not have a financial quantification, but are equally important to recognize.

As can be seen, the impact in this case study equates to a substantial increase. Granted, a portion of this is soft dollars (recovering time, for instance). However, with that increased time, there is also increased capacity of the firm to take on new business without necessarily hiring new people or purchasing new office space or spending more money on technology and equipment. Translating this to a projection over the next several years the figures shown in Table A.3 apply.

TABLE A.3 Sample Estimated Growth of Assets Under Management (AUM)

Year	Target AUM	Goal Benchmarks	Percent
2012	$ 128,266,946	$ —	
2013	$ 168,286,234	$ —	31.2%
2014	$ 220,791,538	$ —	31.2%
2015	$ 289,678,498	$ 250,000,000	31.2%
2016	$ 380,058,190	$ —	31.2%
2017	$ 498,636,345	$ —	31.2%
2018	$ 654,210,885	$ 500,000,000	31.2%
2019	$ 858,324,681	$ —	31.2%
2020	$1,126,121,982	$ —	31.2%
2021	$1,477,472,040	$ 1,000,000,000	31.2%

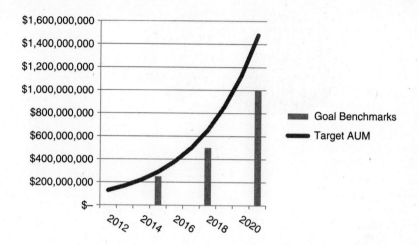

What can be seen from the above chart is that the target AUM actually outstrips the goals established by the firm. This is accomplished through a combination of increased efficiency resulting in increased capacity and substantial cost savings.

About the Companion Website

The companion website has been provided to offer complementary materials to the book. Included in this site you will find:

1. Forms
2. Spreadsheets
3. Flowcharts

We hope you find this information useful. To access the companion website, please go to www.wiley.com/go/efficientpractice. When prompted for a password, please enter "financial."

If you have any further questions or would like help transforming and optimizing your financial practice for greater efficiency and profit, please feel free to visit the author's website: www.efficientpractice.com.

About the Author

Efficient Practice founder and president, Dr. David Lawrence, AIF®, has over 36 years of experience in leadership. He is a veteran of the U.S. Navy during the Vietnam War, having spent over four years on active duty as a noncommissioned officer and later as a commissioned officer in the Naval Reserves. His service in two war zones, first in South Vietnam near the end of the Vietnam War and later in the Middle East, provides a courageous backdrop to his leadership experiences. His compelling story of military leadership during a time of domestic political unrest is truly inspirational.

Dr. Lawrence is a graduate of the University of South Florida in Tampa, with double undergraduate and Master's degrees (cum laude). He attended the University of Florida in Gainesville for his doctorate in Social Behaviorism.

David then spent 18 years with a major financial planning firm as a senior financial advisor, training manager, and district manager. He has also worked for two large independent financial planning and asset management companies in senior management positions. His responsibilities have included managing large numbers of employees as well as setting up employee hiring, training, evaluation, and compensation systems. His background and experience in integrating technological systems with management needs has given him a unique perspective on the use of technology as a leadership tool.

David has spent the past several years writing and speaking. He founded the Efficient Practice, a consulting company devoted to growth efficiency solutions for financial services institutions and their reps. His speaking engagements have taken him all across the United States, Canada, and the Far East. Conversant in five languages, he is acutely aware of and sensitive to the need for efficient communications in leadership and in life.

David is a current member of the International Speakers' Network (ISN). A partial list of David's speaking engagements includes:

- IBM
- U.S. Department of Veterans Affairs (Veterans Administration)
- Financial Advisor Symposium, Chicago

- Financial Advisor Retirement Symposium, Las Vegas
- Financial Planning Association
- Securities Industry Association (now called SIFMA)
- National Association of Variable Annuities (NAVA)
- International Association of Registered Financial Consultants (IARFC)
- Society of Financial Service Professionals (SFSP)
- Financial Professionals Education Expo
- Laserfiche Institute Conference
- National Advisors Trust Shareholder Conference
- TDAmeritrade Institutional National Conference, Schwab Impact Conference
- Financial Services Institute (FSI), *Forbes* Advisor eConference
- Million Dollar Round Table (MDRT) Annual Meeting
- MultiFinancial Connect Conference
- Financial Network Connect Conference
- Technology Tools for Today Conference

He has been frequently quoted by such national publications as *Barron's*, *Financial Planning Interactive*, *USA Today*, and the *Wall Street Journal Online*, among others. He has written articles for *Practice Lifecycle*, the *Investment Management Consultants Association (IMCA) Monitor*, the *Virtual Office* newsletter, and *Turning Point Inc.* newsletter. He has also made frequent appearances on NBC and FOX television affiliates. He is a sought-after public speaker on a variety of leadership, financial, and technical topics. He is a past president of the Financial Planning Association of Tampa Bay and is active in that organization on a national level as past-chair of the FPA's National Leadership Council. Further, David Lawrence was the chair of the FPA's 2006 National Leadership Conference. David currently is a monthly columnist and contributing editor for *Financial Advisor* magazine (www.fa-mag.com). Mr. Lawrence carries the coveted professional designations of Accredited Investment Fiduciary (AIF®).

Index